Introduction to IoT with Machine Learning and Image Processing using Raspberry Pi

Introduction to IoT with Machine Learning and Image Processing using Raspberry Pi

Shrirang Ambaji Kulkarni
Varadraj P. Gurupur
Steven L. Fernandes

CRC Press
Taylor & Francis Group
Boca Raton London New York

CRC Press is an imprint of the
Taylor & Francis Group, an **informa** business

A CHAPMAN & HALL BOOK

MATLAB® is a trademark of The MathWorks, Inc. and is used with permission. The MathWorks does not warrant the accuracy of the text or exercises in this book. This book's use or discussion of MATLAB® software or related products does not constitute endorsement or sponsorship by The MathWorks of a particular pedagogical approach or particular use of the MATLAB® software.

First edition published 2020
by CRC Press
6000 Broken Sound Parkway NW, Suite 300, Boca Raton, FL 33487-2742

and by CRC Press
2 Park Square, Milton Park, Abingdon, Oxon, OX14 4RN

© 2020 Taylor & Francis Group, LLC

CRC Press is an imprint of Taylor & Francis Group, LLC

International Standard Book Number-13: 978-1-138-54352-2 (Hardback)
International Standard Book Number-13: 978-0-367-49373-8 (Paperback)
International Standard Book Number-13: 978-1-351-00666-8 (eBook)

Contents

Authors, vii

CHAPTER 1 ▪ Introduction   1

CHAPTER 2 ▪ Raspberry Pi Unraveled   7

CHAPTER 3 ▪ Python and Its Libraries for Machine Learning   19

CHAPTER 4 ▪ Machine Learning   81

CHAPTER 5 ▪ Introduction to Image Processing   125

BIBLIOGRAPHY, 151

INDEX, 153

Authors

Dr. Shrirang Ambaji Kulkarni is a prolific learner, author, and faculty member with 18-plus years of experience in the field of Computer Science and Engineering. He is currently working as an Associate Professor at the National Institute of Engineering in the Department of Computer Science and Engineering, Mysore, India.

Dr. Varadraj P. Gurupur is an distinguished faculty member and researcher in the field of Health Informatics. He has authored many research articles in reputed journals. He is currently working as an Associate Professor at the University of Central Florida in the Department of Health Informatics, Florida, USA.

Dr. Steven Lawrence Fernandes is a high-profile researcher in the field of Image Processing. He is currently working as Post-Doctoral Fellow at the University of Central Florida in the Department of Computer Science and Engineering, Florida, USA.

## CHAPTER 1

Introduction

I n the last three decades, technology has changed the way we live our lives. This happens to be a universally accepted truth. In this book, we attempt to illustrate the use of a new technology that has changed the world of communication, computing and computing education. Interestingly, the name of this technology coincides with that of a famous dessert named Raspberry Pie. Raspberry *Pi* is a single board computer developed in the United Kingdom. Incidentally, the organization that started this is known as the Raspberry Pi Foundation. This was first launched in the year 2012.

By the year 2015, Raspberry Pi had gained wide-scale popularity. One of the key features of this technology was its size and adaptability. In some strange ways, Raspberry Pi was the panacea the world of technology was dreaming of. To build on this idea of a tiny computer, one must consider the fact that more than a decade ago you would have computer programs running on desktops wired to electromechanical systems that would use them. The advent of the Raspberry Pi enables the community of technology developers to innovate handheld devices than can encompass the power of regular computers. Our intention in writing this book is twofold: a) we want to provide a basic understanding of how a Raspberry Pi can be used for simple applications, and b) we want to provide fundamental information on how a Raspberry Pi can be used to advance innovations in machine learning and image recognition.

While providing fundamental information on Raspberry Pi, we will help students comprehend the necessary information required to develop applications and devices. These devices and applications can have a wide range of applications such as networking devices, using devices and applications related to privacy and security, creating medical applications and developing sensors. The authors believe that this range of applications will help the scientific community adapt Raspberry Pi for use in some of their projects and thereby enhance its usability.

Additionally, the authors are attempting to present information on how Raspberry Pi can successfully implement machine learning and image processing. The information presented in this book will help the community of researchers synthesize new scientific methods, algorithms, devices and other forms of technology into a wide range of application domains. The authors envision Raspberry Pi advancing the development of science and technology across various user domains such as medicine, security, communication, and the military. Last but not least, it is our attempt to have this book used as study material for courses teaching students about using Raspberry Pi. It is our understanding that Raspberry Pi can be used extensively in healthcare information systems.

In this book, the authors present a transformative interdisciplinary perspective of Raspberry Pi usage. This idea is based on the philosophy of transformative transdisciplinary perspective presented by the founding fathers of Society for Design and Process Science [1]. This philosophy is based on bringing about a positive transformative change to one domain by making changes or improvements in another. This philosophy is applicable to Raspberry Pi because rapid improvements in Raspberry Pi and its applicability will facilitate and create a rostrum for improvements in all the domains in which this device can be used. One example will be the implementation of machine learning algorithms that can aid image processing. In this book, the authors have dwelled on some of the fundamental programming concepts that are needed for image analysis and machine learning. This is another very important reason this book is needed for its targeted audience.

While we engage ourselves in recognizing the importance of the Raspberry Pi, it is also important to note that Raspberry Pi has competitors or alternatives available in the market. A brief summary of these alternatives is listed in Table 1.1.

This book is divided into five chapters. The first chapter provides some introductory material on Raspberry Pi and a brief introduction to the

TABLE 1.1   A List of Raspberry Pi Alternatives Available as of 2019 [2]

Raspberry Pi Model	Brief Description
Odroid XU4	Compatible with a few prominent versions of Linux operating system and comparable to Raspberry Pi 3
UDOO Bolt	Works well with desktop applications
ASUS Tinker Board	Works with versions of Linux operating system and Chrome
LattePanda Alpha	Unlike many alternatives; supports windows 10 and uses an Intel Core M3 processor
Banana Pi M64	Works with a wider range of operating systems
RockPro 64	A powerful 64 bit CPU
BeagleBone Black	Developed by Texas Instruments in collaboration with Newark element 14
Libre Computer AML-S905X-CC Le Potato	Suitable for image processing
MinnowBoard Turbot	Its small size and affordability make it a viable competitor for the Raspberry Pi.
Odroid H2	Suitable for game streaming and video applications
Arduino	Useful for applications involving robotics

authors. The second chapter explains different types of Raspberry Pis and provides the reader with important information on the slots and other necessary elements of the Raspberry Pi. An explanation on these elements or parts is essential from a usability perspective. It also provides instructions on installing the operating system Raspbian [3] on Raspberry Pi. Additionally, it provides some information on peripheral devices and the ways in which they can be used with the Raspberry Pi.

The importance of using Raspbian dwells in the idea that installing and using this operating system is a necessary step in the synthesis of systems and applications. Raspbian is a freely available operating system for the Raspberry Pi. It is important to note that Raspbian is not affiliated with the Raspberry Pi Foundation. Raspbian is a community-funded development effort as was the case in the early days of the Linux operating system. Interestingly, Raspbian is a Linux distribution built with the Linux operating system. Raspbian was first released in the year 2012.

The third chapter explains the elements of Python programming [4] that are essential with respect to using Raspberry Pi. Here the authors dwell on esoteric programming details that are needed for successful Raspberry Pi application. These details include matrix operations, Cholesky decomposition and modifying data frames. It is important to note that data manipulation and analysis have become critical in today's world of artificial intelligence and big data. Raspberry Pi provides the much-needed hardware for manipulating big data. The authors understand this need and provide some basic information on the development of systems for data manipulation using the Raspberry Pi. Chapter 3 contains necessary program snippets with illustrations of expected outcomes. One of the critical objectives of this illustration is to help the reader with machine learning application development using the Raspberry Pi. These applications can be applied to smart phones, wearable devices, farming devices and other IoT applications.

Chapter 4 dwells on details with respect to programming machine-learning systems. The authors explore required approaches for splitting data sets into test and training sets essential for machine learning algorithm implementations. We use health informatics examples to explain how machine learning can be implemented using the Raspberry Pi. This chapter provides the reader with necessary information on synthesizing expert systems, developing knowledge banks and performing knowledge curation.

Machine learning implementation is explained with several examples, programing snippets and figures associated with the outcome of their implementation. Implementation of machine learning is important in many domains including health informatics, where machine learning has been extensively used to predict healthcare outcomes and diagnoses and for genetics and bioinformatics. Machine learning and big data analytics have been helpful in predicting the early onset of diseases. Additionally, the possibility of the development of a disease or disorder later in life can be predicted with the application of bioinformatics based on the information derived from human genomes. The integration of Raspberry Pi into portable biomedical devices enhances the possibility of computation.

Finally, chapter 5 deals with image processing using the Raspberry Pi. Here the authors provide many program snippets and associated outputs, thereby delineating details that are necessary for the reader to use the device to perform image-processing algorithms. In recent times, it has been observed that image processing and machine learning associate well. Thus, the authors provide information on machine learning and image processing in this book. With the advent of the Raspberry Pi, the size of the computational device for image processing is reduced while at the same time it improved the available computability. This aids the development and synthesis of real-time sensors in need of advanced processing.

The authors have extensive experience in research and development of science and technology. Dr. Shrirang Kulkarni has a Doctoral degree in Computer Engineering; he started his career in research by exploring and developing technologies for ad hoc wireless networks. He further identified other areas of science and technology in which his fundamental approaches could be used, thereby expanding on the transdisciplinary and transformative nature of his research. He now works on research projects that involve using the Raspberry Pi for developing machine learning techniques for healthcare. Additionally, Dr. Kulkarni has written several books that have attained national attention in India. It is also important to mention that he has been involved in teaching engineering students for the last 18 years.

Dr. Steven Fernandes is a well-accomplished researcher in the area of Internet of Things (IoT), machine learning, image processing and the design and development of intelligent systems. He has published more than 40 articles in reputable journals. Additionally, he has served as a guest editor for several special issues. Dr. Fernandes has been involved in teaching engineering students in India and the United States for about a decade.

Finally, Dr. Varadraj Prabhu Gurupur is currently serving as an Associate Professor with the Department of Health Management and Informatics at the University of Central Florida. Dr. Gurupur has more than 100 publications, including a book, chapters, journal articles, abstracts, conference papers and published reviews. He has worked on several projects funded by agencies such as the National Science Foundation and the National Institutes of Health. He has been actively involved with the Institute of Electrical and Electronic Engineers for over a decade. Additionally, he has been honored with several national, regional and state level awards in the United States for his accomplishments in the area of Health Informatics. Dr. Gurupur received his Master's in Computer Science in the year 2005 and Doctor of Philosophy in Computer engineering in 2010 from the University of Alabama at Birmingham.

REFERENCES

[1] Society for Design and Process Science Official Website [Online]. Available: www.sdpsnet.org/sdps/. Accessed: 09/24/2019.

[2] Electromaker [Online]. Available: www.electromaker.io/blog/article/10-best-raspberry-pi-alternatives. Accessed: 09/24/2019.

[3] Raspbian [Online]. Available: www.raspbian.org/RaspbianImages

[4] S.A. Kulkarni, *Problem Solving and Python Programming*, YesDee Publishers, Chennai, India, 2017.

## CHAPTER 2

Raspberry Pi Unraveled

2.0 RASPBERRY PI

Raspberry Pi is an Advanced RISC Machines (ARM)-processed, credit-card sized computer. It was developed by the Raspberry Pi Foundation in the United Kingdom (UK).

> ARM stands for Advanced RISC Machines. The company specializes in building processors based on Reduced Instruction Set Computers (RISC) architecture. RISC machines emphasize the use of registers and smaller instructions and thus can achieve higher speeds with the ability to execute millions of instructions per second. The smaller size of ARM processors' low power consumption makes them most suitable for miniaturized devices like the Raspberry Pi.
>
> The latest model (Raspberry Pi 3 B+) uses 1.2 GHz ARM Cortex – A53 Broadcom BCM 2837 Processor. The significant difference is the quad-core ARM Cortex A53 (ARMv8) cluster, which works at 1.2 GHz, making it 50% faster than the Raspberry Pi 2 model.

2.1 TIMELINE OF RASPBERRY PI MODELS

A brief timeline of various base Raspberry Pi models released to date follows.

Year: 2012	Year: 2013
Model: Raspberry Pi Model B	Model: Raspberry Pi Model A
Size: 85.60 mm × 56.5 mm	Size: 85.60 mm × 56.5 mm
CPU: ARM1176JZF-S; 32 bit	CPU: ARM1176JZF-S 32 bit
GPU: Broadcom VideoCore IV @ 250 MHz	GPU: Broadcom VideoCore IV @ 250 MHz
Speed: 700Mhz Single-Core CPU	Speed: 700Mhz Single-Core CPU
RAM: 512MB RAM	RAM: 256 MB RAM

Year: 2014	Year: 2015
Model: Raspberry Pi Compute model	Model: Raspberry Pi Zero
Size: 67.6 mm × 30 mm	Size: 65 mm × 30 mm × 5 mm
CPU: ARM1176JZF-S 32 bit	CPU: ARM1176JZF-S 32 bit
GPU: Broadcom VideoCore IV @ 250 MHz	GPU: Broadcom VideoCore IV @ 250 MHz
Speed: 700Mhz Single-Core CPU	Speed: 1 GHz Single-Core CPU
RAM: 512 MB RAM	RAM: 512 MB RAM

Latest Raspberry Pi Model

Year: 2018
Model: **Raspberry Pi 3 Model B+**
Size: 85mm x 56mm x 17mm.
CPU: Cortex-A53 (ARMv8) 64-bit
GPU: Dual Core VideoCore IV GPU@400 MHz
Speed: 1.4GHz 64-bit quad-core ARM Cortex A53 CPU
RAM: 1GB RAM

2.2 COMPONENTS OF A RASPBERRY PI MODEL 3

A brief component layout of Raspberry Pi Model 3 is illustrated in Figure 2.1. The model we considered in this book is Raspberry Pi 3 V 1.2

2.2.1 General Purpose Input-Output Pins (GPIO) Pins

There are 40 general purpose input-output pins (GPIO) pins on the Raspberry Pi board as illustrated in Figure 2.2. These pins help the Raspberry Pi connect to the real world. With the help of these pins, the Raspberry Pi can help you control physical devices like motors, extension boards and LEDs.

The pins on the left side of the board are numbered using odd numbers from 1 to 39; the right side uses even numbers from 2 to 40. The GPIO pins are numbered in two nomenclatures. One is the GPIO numbering

FIGURE 2.1   Raspberry Pi Model 3.

FIGURE 2.2   GPIO Pins.

and the other is the physical numbering. The GPIO numbering refers to the Broadcom numbering on System on Chip, whereas the physical numbering refers to the 40 pins specified on the Raspberry Pi Board.

2.2.2 Broadcom BCM283 7 64bit ARMv7 Quad Core Processor

At the center of the Raspberry Pi is an ARMv7 Quad Core Processor with 1GB of RAM, which works at 1.2 GHz. The miniature size of the processor is noticeable. The Quad-Core nature of the processor at the rate of 1.2 Ghz makes it 50% faster than the Raspberry Pi 2. Coupled with GPU, the Raspberry Pi can work wonders in number-crunching situations.

2.2.3 Micro USB Slot

The Micro USB power connector supplies power to the Raspberry Pi board. This is illustrated in Figure 2.3.

The Raspberry Pi board is powered by 5v DC supply. To turn the Raspberry Pi on/off you need to turn this power supply on/off.

2.2.4 High Definition Multimedia Interface (HDMI) Port

The Raspberry Pi provides a high definition multimedia interface (HDMI) output port. This is illustrated in Figure 2.4.

The HDMI port allows the Raspberry Pi to connect to a monitor. For monitors that support only o video graphics array (VGA) you need an HDMI to VGA connector cable. With the support from GPU, the Raspberry Pi can support 1080p video and that could be truly outputted from an HDMI port.

2.2.5 Audio Jack

For listening to sound, the Raspberry Pi provides a 3.5 mm audio jack. This is illustrated in Figure 2.5. You can plug earphones into this audio jack.

FIGURE 2.3   Micro USB Slot.

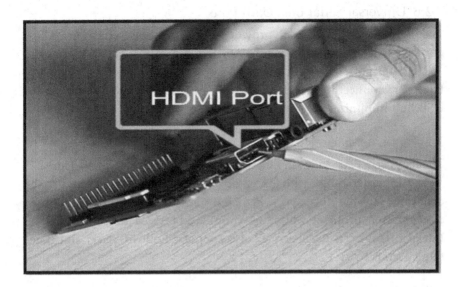

FIGURE 2.4   HDMI Port.

FIGURE 2.5   Audio Jack/Port.

2.2.6 Universal Serial Bus (USB) Ports

The Raspberry Pi 3 model provides four universal serial bus (USB) ports. This is illustrated in Figure 2.6.

The USB ports allow for the connection of a mouse and a keyboard. However, connecting devices indirectly to the Raspberry Pi through a USB hub minimizes the power drawn.

2.2.7 Ethernet Socket

The Raspberry Pi provides an Ethernet socket. This is illustrated in Figure 2.7.

The Ethernet cable, with its RJ-45 connector, allows a router to be connected to the Raspberry Pi. Thus, a router with dynamic host configuration protocol will allow your Raspberry Pi to connect to the Internet. However, Raspberry Pi also supports built-in Wi-Fi and Bluetooth connectivity.

2.2.8 Micro-SD Card Slot

Raspberry Pi provides an onboard micro-SD card slot. This is illustrated in Figure 2.8.

FIGURE 2.6   USB Ports.

FIGURE 2.7   Ethernet Port.

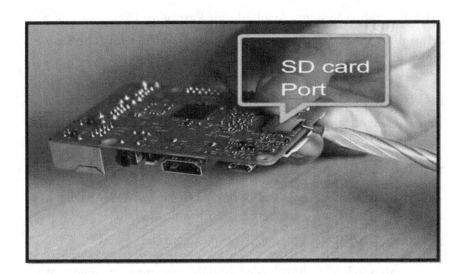

FIGURE 2.8   SD Card Port.

For the Raspberry to boot through its operating system, it needs the operating system to reside on the SD card. This is essential, as Raspberry Pi does not have a hard-drive like in a laptop or desktop.

2.3 RASPBIAN OPERATING SYSTEM

The soul of a computer system is its operating system. The preferred operating system for Raspberry Pi is Raspbian. Raspbian is based on Debian, which is a Linux-based operating system highly customized for Raspberry Pi hardware. The popular versions of Raspberry Pi are Wheezy, which is based on Debian 7, Jessie, which is based on Debian 8, and Stretch, based on Debian 9. The operating system considered in this book is Jessie.

The Jessie version of Raspberry Pi focused on making the desktop more comfortable for end users. The LibreOffice suite was included in the Jessie version. This helps users write documents, prepare PowerPoints and work with Excel spreadsheets and databases. All of these are compatible with Microsoft Windows. The Jessie version comes bundled with BlueJ, a Java development environment for beginners, and Scratch, a programming language for beginners. The graphical user interface provided for Raspbian is the Lightweight Desktop Environment or LXDE.

2.3.1 Operating Systems Available for Raspberry Pi

Let us discuss some of the operating systems available for Raspberry Pi, shown in Table 2.1.

2.4 TO CONNECT RASPBERRY PI 3 TO MONITOR

Step 1: Connect a monitor to Raspberry Pi via HDMI and a keyboard and mouse via a USB.

Step 2: Install an Operating System.

> **Step 2.1:** Use new out-of-box software (NOOBs) available at (https://www.raspberrypi.org/downloads/).
>
> **Step 2.2:** Extract the NOOBs downloaded.
>
> **Step 2.3:** The downloaded NOOBS file must be copied into a formatted SD card. (SDHC card >2GB and ≤ = 32 GB follows FAT 32). NOOBs will install Raspbian on the SD card at the initial boot.

TABLE 2.1   Operating System supporting Raspberry Pi

Raspbian

- Raspberry Pi Foundation recommended OS
- A very user friendly desktop environment
- Comes with a lot of pre-installed software

LibreELEC

- Designed to support Kodi-powered media center
- Can be paired with the KODI Remote App
- Can build a small home theater

Windows 10 IoT Core

- Provides integration with Visual Studio
- Supports both ARM and X86 architectures
- Supports development of connected devices

RISC OS

- Performance is key and is emphasized by the designers
- Comes with an archived file, which is unto 4MB, a very small size
- Provides better drag-and-drop options

Step 3: raspi-config
$ sudo raspi-config

You will see the following screen (Figure 2.9). Choose the interfacing options.

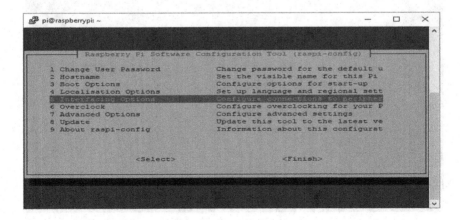

FIGURE 2.9   Choosing Interfacing Options.

Press Enter to move into an option and arrow keys to move up/down. Tab to select the options like <finish>.

Step 3.1: Change the user password. The default login is **pi** and password is **raspberry**.

Step 3.2: Enable boot to Desktop.

Step 3.3: Internationalization options

Step 3.3.1: Change-locale: select a language.

Step 3.3.2: Change time zone.

Step 3.3.3: Change keyboard layout. QWERTY is the default.

Post successful configuration; the Raspberry Pi environment will look as shown in Figure 2.10.

FIGURE 2.10   Raspberry Pi Desktop.

2.5 APPLICATIONS OF IOT

According to Gartner[1], by 2020 there will be around 2.6 billion connected devices. This clearly indicates a potential host of applications.

1. **Smart Home:** The Smart Home is the most potent application for IoT. You can control air conditioners, refrigerators, microwave ovens, lighting and entertainment systems through IoT-based control systems.

2. **Wearable devices:** Monitoring human health parameters like heartbeat, blood pressure and other vitals is possible through wearable IoT devices. The constraint on these devices is that they must be small and energy efficient.

3. **Farming:** Farmers are at times challenged to monitor crops and livestock at remote farm areas. Now this is possible through IoT. Also, detecting diseases of crops and water usage can be controlled through IoT devices.

4. **Industrial IoT:** It has been now realized that IoT has a host of applications across different industries like manufacturing, oil and gas and energy. IoT helps industries in the automation and optimization of resources.

EXERCISES

1. Show how to make a headless Raspberry Pi installation.

2. Explain why Secure Shell (SSH) is disabled from Raspberry Pi 3 onwards.

3. What type of file system is preferred on the SD card used for uploading the Raspberry Pi operating system?

4. Discuss the various operating systems available for Raspberry Pi along with their advantages and disadvantages.

5. Write a note on the most recent industrial applications of Raspberry Pi as Industrial IoT.

REFERENCE

[1] Gartner, https://www.gartner.com/en/newsroom/press-releases/2019-08-29-gartner-says-5-8-billion-enterprise-and-automotive-io, 2019.

## CHAPTER 3

Python and Its Libraries for Machine Learning

3.1 INTRODUCTION

Python is one of the most popular languages for Machine Learning. One of the dominant reasons for the popularity of Python is its rich support of libraries (see Table 3.1).

TABLE 3.1   Libraries for Python

Python Library	Usage
NumPy	Mathematical applications
SciPy	Scientifics Computing
Pandas	Data Analysis
Matplotib	Data Visualization
Scikit-learn	Machine Learning

3.2 PYTHON

3.2.1 What Is Python?

- Python was proposed by Guido van Rossum in the late 1980s.

- It is a simple but powerful high-level programming language.

- It supports procedural and object-oriented concepts.

- Python code is interpreted rather than compiled.

3.3 A TYPICAL PYTHON PROGRAM

```
File  Edit  Format  Run  Options  Windows  Help

'''
Python program to print square root of every elemment in a given matrix
'''
import sys  #import system module
import math #import math module
print("Enter the dimensions of matrix on a single line ")
m,n = map(int, sys.stdin.readline().split())
print("Enter the values of the first matrix: ")
A=[]
A=[[0 for x in range(m)]for y in range(n)]
for i in range(0,m):    #for loop
    for j in range(0,n):
        A[i][j]=int(input())
print("The entered matrix is: ") #print statement in Python
for i in range(len(A)):
    for j in range(len(A[0])):
        print((A[i][j]),end=' ')
    print()
print("Square root of every element of  a matrix: ")
C=[]
C=[[0 for x in range(m)]for y in range(n)]
for i in range(len(A)):
    for j in range(len(C[0])):
        C[i][j]=math.sqrt(A[i][j])
for i in range(len(C)):
    for j in range(len(C[0])):
        print((C[i][j]),"\t\t\t",end='')
    print()
```
```
                                                    Ln: 30 Col: 0
```

FIGURE 3.1   A Typical Python Program.

```
File  Edit  Shell  Debug  Options  Windows  Help

Python 3.4.2 (default, Sep 26 2018, 07:16:01)
[GCC 4.9.2] on linux
Type "copyright", "credits" or "license()" for more information.
>>> ============================== RESTART ==============================
>>>
Enter the dimensions of matrix on a single line
2 2
Enter the values of the first matrix:
1
2
3
4
The entered matrix is:
1 2
3 4
Square root of every element of  a matrix:
1.0                     1.4142135623730951
1.7320508075688772                      2.0
>>>
```
```
                                                    Ln: 19 Col: 4
```

FIGURE 3.2   Output of a Typical Python Program.

Thus, we now see a typical Python program, which computes the square root of every element of a given matrix. A Python program typically begins with an import statement. The import statement includes Python modules that provide a programmer with various library functions. In the mentioned program we have used library functions like map(), split() and sqrt(). Python follows strict rules for code indentation. The inner for loop is indented a few more spaces than the outer for loop is.

3.4 PYTHON KEYWORDS

Keywords are reserved words and cannot be used as names for identifiers or programmer-defined variables. The keywords are listed in the **keyword** module and can be printed as seen in Figure 3.3.

```
File  Edit  Shell  Debug  Options  Windows  Help
Python 3.4.2 (default, Sep 26 2018, 07:16:01)
[GCC 4.9.2] on linux
Type "copyright", "credits" or "license()" for more information.
>>> import keyword
>>> print(keyword.kwlist)
['False', 'None', 'True', 'and', 'as', 'assert', 'break', 'class', 'continue'
, 'def', 'del', 'elif', 'else', 'except', 'finally', 'for', 'from', 'global',
'if', 'import', 'in', 'is', 'lambda', 'nonlocal', 'not', 'or', 'pass', 'raise
', 'return', 'try', 'while', 'with', 'yield']
>>>
                                                                    Ln: 7 Col: 4
```

FIGURE 3.3   Python Code to Display Keyword List.

3.5 PYTHON VARIABLE

- A python variable must begin with a letter (a – z, A – B) or underscore (_) followed by letters, numbers or underscore.

- Python variables are case sensitive.

mean	⟵	valid variable
1_mean	⟵	invalid variable
mean_new@	⟵	invalid variable
_new_mean	⟵	valid variable

3.6 COMMENTS IN PYTHON

Python provides two types of comments. This is as shown as comments. py in Figure 3.4.

```
File  Edit  Format  Run  Options  Windows  Help
'''
This is a multiline comment in Python.
It can be used to briefly describe Python programs.
'''
#This is a single line comment
print("Comments in Python")

                                                              Ln: 8 Col: 0
```

FIGURE 3.4   Python Program to Demonstrate Comments.

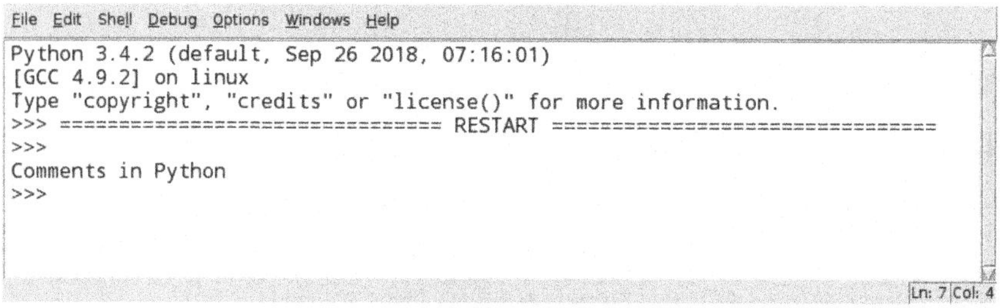

```
File  Edit  Shell  Debug  Options  Windows  Help
Python 3.4.2 (default, Sep 26 2018, 07:16:01)
[GCC 4.9.2] on linux
Type "copyright", "credits" or "license()" for more information.
>>> ============================== RESTART ==============================
>>>
Comments in Python
>>>

                                                              Ln: 7 Col: 4
```

FIGURE 3.5   Output of comments.py.

In Figure 3.5, we observe that comments are ignored by the Python interpreter.

3.7 PYTHON DATA TYPES

Variables in Python are typeless. Python supports dynamic typing, and the variable type is decided at runtime Python data types can be categorized as shown in Table 3.2.

TABLE 3.2   Python data types

Python Data Types

Numeric	int
	long
	float
	complex
	bool
Sequence	str
	list
	tuple
Sets	set
	frozen set
Mapping	dict

To determine the data type of the variable use the **type()** function in Python. **Python program: datatype.py** as illustrated in Figure 3.6.

```
File  Edit  Format  Run  Options  Windows  Help
a=827
b=12345678
c=23.47
d=True
e=8+9j
f="Hello"
g=[1,2,3,4,5,6,7]
h=(1,2,3,4,5,6,7)
i=set("Welcome to Python")
j={'a':'I','b':'Like','c':'Python','d':'Programming'}
print("a: ",a, "------>",type(a))
print("b: ",b, "------>",type(b))
print("c: ",c, "------>",type(c))
print("d: ",d, "------>",type(d))
print("e: ",e, "------>",type(e))
print("f: ",f, "------>",type(f))
print("g: ",g, "------>",type(g))
print("h: ",h, "------>",type(h))
print("i: ",i, "------>",type(i))
print("j: ",j, "------>",type(j))

                                                        Ln: 22 Col: 0
```

FIGURE 3.6   Python Program to Demonstrate Different Data Types.

```
File  Edit  Shell  Debug  Options  Windows  Help
Python 3.4.2 (default, Sep 26 2018, 07:16:01)
[GCC 4.9.2] on linux
Type "copyright", "credits" or "license()" for more information.
>>> ============================== RESTART ==============================
>>>
a:  827 ------> <class 'int'>
b:  12345678 ------> <class 'int'>
c:  23.47 ------> <class 'float'>
d:  True ------> <class 'bool'>
e:  (8+9j) ------> <class 'complex'>
f:  Hello ------> <class 'str'>
g:  [1, 2, 3, 4, 5, 6, 7] ------> <class 'list'>
h:  (1, 2, 3, 4, 5, 6, 7) ------> <class 'tuple'>
i:  {'e', 'P', ' ', 'n', 'W', 'l', 't', 'y', 'c', 'm', 'h', 'o'} ------> <class 'set'>
j:  {'a': 'I', 'd': 'Programming', 'c': 'Python', 'b': 'Like'} ------> <class 'dict'>
>>>
                                                                        Ln: 16 Col: 4
```

FIGURE 3.7   Output of datatype.py.

3.8 PYTHON OPERATOR PRECEDENCE

The Python operator and precedence are given in Table 3.3.

TABLE 3.3   Python Operator Precedence and Associativity

Operator	Highest	Associativity
**		Right-to-left
~ + −		Left-to-right
* / % //		Left-to-right
+ −		Left-to-right
>> <<		Left-to-right
&		Left-to-right
^ |		Left-to-right
<= < > >=		Left-to-right
<> == !=		Left-to-right
= %= /= //= −= += *= **=		Right-to-left
is is not		Left-to-right
In not in		Left-to-right
not or and	Lowest	Left-to-right

3.8.1 Evaluate the Following Python Expression

2 + 3 * 4//5 − 17

Step 1: (3*4) = 12

Step 2: 12//5 = 2 (Integer division)

Step 3: 2 + 2 = 4

Step 4: 4–17 = −13

Ans = −13

3.8.2 Evaluate the Following Python Expression

2**3+4//7−6*9

Step 1: (2**3) = 8

Step 2: 4//7 = 0 (Integer division)

Step 3: 6 * 9 = 54

Step 4: 8 + 0 = 8

Step 5: 8–54 = −46

Ans = − 46

3.9 CONDITIONAL CONSTRUCTS IN PYTHON

Conditional constructs are used in Python to take action based on certain conditions. The conditions can involve comparison expressions or arithmetic expressions, and their outcome is either True or False.

Structure of IF-ELSE Statement in Python

```
if condition1:
        statement 1
elif condition2:
        statement 2
else:
        statement 3
```

Example: Consider the following description

    0–1: baby

    1–2: toddler

    2–12: child

    13–17: teenager (14 = early teens)

    18 +: adult

Python program:if_elif_stmt.py is illustrated in Figure 3.8.

```
File  Edit  Format  Run  Options  Windows  Help
'''
Python program to demonstrate if elif statement
'''
age = int(input("Please enter a age: ")) #Python input statement
if age>=0 and age<=1: #Python if statement
    print("Baby")
elif age>1 and age <=2: #Python elif statement
    print("Toddler")
elif age>2 and age <=12:
    print("Child")
elif age>12 and age <=17:
    print("Teenager")
else:                    #Python else statement
    print("Adult")


                                                          Ln: 15 Col: 0
```

FIGURE 3.8   Python Program to Demonstrate if elif Statements.

```
File  Edit  Shell  Debug  Options  Windows  Help
Python 3.4.2 (default, Sep 26 2018, 07:16:01)
[GCC 4.9.2] on linux
Type "copyright", "credits" or "license()" for more information.
>>> ============================== RESTART ==============================
>>>
Please enter a age: 6
Child
>>> ============================== RESTART ==============================
>>>
Please enter a age: 19
Adult
>>>

                                                          Ln: 12 Col: 4
```

FIGURE 3.9   Output of Python Program if_elif_stmt.py.

3.10 TERNARY OPERATOR IN PYTHON

The syntax for Python's ternary operator is as follows.

a if test else b

```
File  Edit  Format  Run  Options  Windows  Help
'''
Python ternary operator demo
'''
marks=int(input("Please enter the marks: "))
result = 1 if marks > 35 else 0
if result == 1:
    print("Pass")
else:
    print("Fail")



                                                              Ln: 10 Col: 0
```

FIGURE 3.10   Python Program to Demonstrate Use of Ternary Operator.

```
File  Edit  Shell  Debug  Options  Windows  Help
Python 3.4.2 (default, Sep 26 2018, 07:16:01)
[GCC 4.9.2] on linux
Type "copyright", "credits" or "license()" for more information.
>>> ============================ RESTART ============================
>>>
Please enter the marks: 65
Pass
>>> ============================ RESTART ============================
>>>
Please enter the marks: 34
Fail
>>>

                                                              Ln: 12 Col: 4
```

FIGURE 3.11   Output of Python Program to Demonstrate Ternary Operator.

3.11 LOOPING CONSTRUCTS IN PYTHON

At times when certain statements are to be executed repeatedly, loops are useful. Thus, the statements are executed continuously until some conditions are met.

3.11.1 While Loop

A while loop is an entry-controlled loop. Thus, the loop is entered only if the entry condition is satisfied. There may be a counter that keeps count of the number of time the loop is executed and finally when a certain threshold is reached, the loop terminates. The syntax is as follows

while expression:
    statement

The while loop iterates as long as the condition is True. The Statement can be a single statement or block of statements.

Example: Python program while_loop.py as seen in Figure 3.12.

```
File  Edit  Format  Run  Options  Windows  Help
'''
demo of while loop in python
'''
friend=True
while friend:
    fight=int(input("Please enter 1 if you have fought or 0 otherwise: "))
    if fight == 1:
        print("Sorry the friendship is in trouble")
        friend=False
    else:
        print("Our friendship is great")
                                                                    Ln: 12 Col: 0
```

FIGURE 3.12   Python Program to Demonstrate while loop.

```
File  Edit  Shell  Debug  Options  Windows  Help
Python 3.4.2 (default, Sep 26 2018, 07:16:01)
[GCC 4.9.2] on linux
Type "copyright", "credits" or "license()" for more information.
>>> ================================ RESTART ================================
>>>
Please enter 1 if you have fought or 0 otherwise: 0
Our friendship is great
Please enter 1 if you have fought or 0 otherwise: 1
Sorry the friendship is in trouble
>>>
                                                                    Ln: 10 Col: 4
```

FIGURE 3.13   Output of while_loop.py.

3.11.2 For Loop

The for loop in Python iterates over a given range of values. The syntax of the for loop is as follows

    for item in sequence:
        print item

Example: Python program – for_loop.py as illustrated in Figure 3.14.

```
File  Edit  Format  Run  Options  Windows  Help
'''
demo of for loop in Python
'''
item = 10
for i in range(0,item):
    print(i)
```
Ln: 7 Col: 0

FIGURE 3.14   Python Program to Demonstrate for_loop.py.

```
File  Edit  Shell  Debug  Options  Windows  Help
Python 3.4.2 (default, Sep 26 2018, 07:16:01)
[GCC 4.9.2] on linux
Type "copyright", "credits" or "license()" for more information.
>>> ================================ RESTART ================================
>>>
0
1
2
3
4
5
6
7
8
9
>>>
```
Ln: 16 Col: 4

FIGURE 3.15   Output of Python Program for_loop.py.

To perform a similar iteration using the for loop in the reverse manner, consider the program for_loop_reverse.py.

```
File  Edit  Format  Run  Options  Windows  Help
'''
Demo of for loop
'''
item=10
for i in range(item-1, -1, -1):
    print(i)
```
Ln: 7 Col: 0

FIGURE 3.16   Python Program to Demonstrate for loop in the Reverse Manner.

```
File Edit Shell Debug Options Windows Help
Python 3.4.2 (default, Sep 26 2018, 07:16:01)
[GCC 4.9.2] on linux
Type "copyright", "credits" or "license()" for more information.
>>> ============================== RESTART ==============================
>>>
9
8
7
6
5
4
3
2
1
0
>>>
```
Ln: 16 Col: 4

FIGURE 3.17   Output of Python Program for_loop_reverse.py.

3.11.3 Else in Combination with While and For Loop

The else condition with while loop activates when the while entry condition become False. For example, consider the Python program illustrated in Figure 3.18.

```
File Edit Format Run Options Windows Help
'''
demo of else with while loop
'''
num=0
print("I am entering while loop")
while num<=5:
    print("Num= ",num)
    num=num+1
else:
    print("I am in the else part")
    print("Num= ",num)
```
Ln: 12 Col: 0

FIGURE 3.18   Python Program to Demonstrate else in Combination with while loop.

```
File Edit Shell Debug Options Windows Help
Python 3.4.2 (default, Sep 26 2018, 07:16:01)
[GCC 4.9.2] on linux
Type "copyright", "credits" or "license()" for more information.
>>> ============================== RESTART ==============================
>>>
I am entering while loop
Num=   0
Num=   1
Num=   2
Num=   3
Num=   4
Num=   5
I am in the else part
Num=   6
>>>
                                                                    Ln: 15 Col: 4
```

FIGURE 3.19   Output of Python Program for else with while loop.

The else statement is clubbed with the for loop in the case in which the for loop has been exhausted by iterating with all elements in the sequence. For example, consider the Python program illustrated in Figure 3.20.

```
File Edit Format Run Options Windows Help
'''
demo of for loop with else in Python
'''
primes=[2,3,5,7,11]
print("In FOR loop")
for prime in primes:
    print("Prime number: ",prime)
else:
    print("In Else part")
    print("Prime numbers are exhausted")
                                                                    Ln: 11 Col: 0
```

FIGURE 3.20   Python Program to Demonstrate else in Combination with for loop.

```
File Edit Shell Debug Options Windows Help
Python 3.4.2 (default, Sep 26 2018, 07:16:01)
[GCC 4.9.2] on linux
Type "copyright", "credits" or "license()" for more information.
>>> ============================== RESTART ==============================
>>>
In FOR loop
Prime number:   2
Prime number:   3
Prime number:   5
Prime number:   7
Prime number:   11
In Else part
Prime numbers are exhausted
>>>
                                                                    Ln: 14 Col: 4
```

FIGURE 3.21   Output of Python Program for Else with for loop.

3.12 STRINGS IN PYTHON

Strings are contiguous set of characters enclosed by double quotes in Python.

Example: "Hello"
"Raju"

The concatenation of two strings is performed with the "+" operator. Example a = "Good" and b = "Morning". Then a+ b will give Good Morning.

The operator "in" returns True if the given character is in the string. The operator "not in" returns True if the given character is not in the given string. Example G in Good returns True and G not in Morning returns True.

3.12.1 String Built-in Methods

Following are some of the commonly used string methods

a. **len(string)** returns the length of the string.
   Example: len("morning")
   Output: 7

b. **lower()** converts uppercase letters into lowercase.
   Example: str= "HELLO"
            print str.lower()
   Output: hello

c. **find()** finds whether the string is there in a string or in a substring of the string.
   find(sub, start = 0, end = len(string))
   Example: str= "morning"
            str.find("r",0,len(str))
   Output: 2

d. **replace()** replaces the old string with a new string and returns the updated string.
   replace(old, new, max_occurrence)
   Example: str="Good Morning"
            str.replace("Morning", "Evening",1)
   Output: 'Good Evening'

e. **split()** method provides a way to split a string into small substrings separated by a delimiter. The output is a list.

Example: str="Winning is everything"

str.split()

Output: ['Winning', 'is', 'everything']

3.13 LIST IN PYTHON

A list is comma-delimited values enclosed in square brackets. Example lst = ['a', 'b', 'c', 'd']. The Python program list_op.py illustrates in Figure 3.22 an example of list.

```
File  Edit  Format  Run  Options  Windows  Help
'''
Python program to demonstrate a list
'''
lst=['a','b','c',1,2]
for item in lst:
    if str(item).isdigit():
        print("Item: ",item," is a digit")
    else:
        print("Item: ",item," is a char")

                                              Ln: 10 Col: 0
```

FIGURE 3.22   Python Program to Demonstrate an Example of list.

```
File  Edit  Shell  Debug  Options  Windows  Help
Python 3.4.2 (default, Sep 26 2018, 07:16:01)
[GCC 4.9.2] on linux
Type "copyright", "credits" or "license()" for more information.
>>> ================================ RESTART ================================
>>>
Item:  a  is a char
Item:  b  is a char
Item:  c  is a char
Item:  1  is a digit
Item:  2  is a digit
>>>
                                              Ln: 11 Col: 4
```

FIGURE 3.23   Output of Python Program list_op.py.

3.13.1 List Methods

- **len(list)** gives the length of the list.

lst=['a', 'b', 'c', 'd']

len(lst)

Output: 4

- **list.reverse()** reverses the elements of the list.
  lst=['a', 'b', 'c', 'd']
  lst.reverse()
  lst=['d', 'c', 'b', 'a']

- **list.sort()** sorts the elements of the list in ascending order.
  lst=['d', 'c', 'b', 'a']
  lst.sort()
  lst= ['a', 'b', 'c', 'd']

3.14 TUPLES IN PYTHON

Tuples are sequences similar to lists except that they are immutable (i.e., they cannot be changed and they use parentheses). Example tup= ('a', 'b', 'c', 'd')

- **len(tuple)** gives the length of the tuple.
  tup=('a', 'b', 'c', 'd')
  len(tup)
  4

- **max(tuple)** returns the max value in a tuple.
  tup=(1,2,3,4)
  max(tup)
  4

- **min(tuple)** returns the min value of the tuple.
  tup=(1,2,3,4)
  min(tup)
  1

3.15 DICTIONARIES IN PYTHON

Dictionaries are key value pairs separated by ":" and enclosed in curly braces. Example dict ={'a': 'apple', 'b': 'ball', 'c': 'cat', 'd': 'dog', 'e': 'elephant'}

3.15.1 Methods on Dictionaries

- **dict.items()** returns dictionary as key/value pairs.
  print dict.items()
  [('a', 'apple'), ('c', 'cat'), ('b', 'ball'), ('e', 'elephant'), ('d', 'dog')]

- **dict.keys()** returns the dictionary's keys only.
  print dict.keys()
  ['a', 'c', 'b', 'e', 'd']

- **dict.values()** returns the dictionary's values only.
  print dict.values()
  ['apple', 'cat', 'ball', 'elephant', 'dog']

3.16 PYTHON FUNCTIONS

A user-defined function in Python is defined with the def keyword. A function can accept parameters and return a value.

```
File  Edit  Format  Run  Options  Windows  Help
def sum_two(a,b): #user defined function definition
    c = a + b
    return c

x=int(input("Enter the value of x: "))
y=int(input("Enter the value of y: "))
s=sum_two(x,y)
print("Sum of ",x," and ",y,"is ",s)

                                          Ln: 10 Col: 0
```

FIGURE 3.24 Python Program to Demonstrate a Function That Can Accept and Return a Value.

```
File  Edit  Shell  Debug  Options  Windows  Help
Python 3.4.2 (default, Sep 26 2018, 07:16:01)
[GCC 4.9.2] on linux
Type "copyright", "credits" or "license()" for more information.
>>> ============================ RESTART ============================
>>>
Enter the value of x: 10
Enter the value of y: 20
Sum of  10  and  20 is  30
>>>

                                          Ln: 9 Col: 4
```

FIGURE 3.25 Output of Python Function Program.

3.17 NUMPY INTRODUCTION

NumPy is an abbreviation that stands for numerical python. It is a fundamental python package useful for performing data analysis and supporting machine-learning algorithms. As datasets for machine learning algorithms come from a variety of sources and follow different formats, it becomes quite challenging to process the same. These datasets may include images, text or sound clips. These data sources for processing are visualized as numerical arrays. Thus, NumPy as a python package supports huge capabilities for array processing. NumPy also provides the following functionalities:

- ndarray, which supports high-dimensional arrays with superior performance capabilities.

- Mathematical functions to support operations on entire arrays as a single unit.

It provides support for linear algebra operations and allows Python code to interact with C and C++.

How to use NumPy

The convention is to use NumPy with the command as illustrated in Figure 3.26.

```
File  Edit  Shell  Debug  Options  Windows  Help
Python 3.4.2 (default, Sep 26 2018, 07:16:01)
[GCC 4.9.2] on linux
Type "copyright", "credits" or "license()" for more information.
>>> import numpy as np
>>>
                                                        Ln: 5 Col: 4
```

FIGURE 3.26 Usage of NumPy module.

If you see the above screen, the execution of **import numpy as np** resulted in the interpreter prompt >>>; this means that the NumPy package is installed correctly.

3.18 NUMPY OPERATIONS

3.18.1 Creating an Array from a Python List

The first step is to build a Python list. Let us consider lst=[10, 20, 30, 40, 50]. To convert the list to an array we have to use the function np.array () and pass the argument to the list (i.e., lst). This is visualized in Figure 3.27.

```
File Edit Shell Debug Options Windows Help
Python 3.4.2 (default, Sep 26 2018, 07:16:01)
[GCC 4.9.2] on linux
Type "copyright", "credits" or "license()" for more information.
>>> import numpy as np
>>> lst=[10,20,30,40,50]
>>> np.array(lst)
array([10, 20, 30, 40, 50])
>>>
                                                          Ln: 8 Col: 4
```

FIGURE 3.27   Python Command Code to Create an Array from Python List.

NumPy requires that all array elements be of the same type. If the elements do not match, the lower type will be converted or promoted to a higher type.

```
File Edit Shell Debug Options Windows Help
Python 3.4.2 (default, Sep 26 2018, 07:16:01)
[GCC 4.9.2] on linux
Type "copyright", "credits" or "license()" for more information.
>>> import numpy as np
>>> lst=[10.1, 20.2, 30, 40, 50]
>>> np.array(lst)
array([ 10.1, 20.2, 30. , 40. , 50. ])
>>>
                                                          Ln: 8 Col: 4
```

FIGURE 3.28   Python Command Code to Show Type Conversion When Creating an Array from Python List.

Some of the basic datatypes supported by NumPy are illustrated in Table 3.4.

TABLE 3.4 NumPy data types

DataType	Description
bool_	Boolean True or False
int32	Supports Integers on 32 bit machines
int64	Supports Integers on 64 bit machines
uint32	Supports unsigned integer (0 to 4,294,967,295)
Uint64	Supports unsigned integer(0 to 18,446,744,073,709,551,615)
float32	Single precision floating point value
float64	Double precision floating point value
intc	Equivalent to int32 or int64
floatc	Equivalent to float64
complex64	Supports complex number where both real and imaginary parts are 32-bit floats.
Complex128	Supports complex number where both real and imaginary parts are 64-bit floats.

Suppose we want to create a list of integers to float64: we can use the keyword dtype= 'float64'. This is executed as illustrated in Figure 3.29.

```
File  Edit  Shell  Debug  Options  Windows  Help
Python 3.4.2 (default, Sep 26 2018, 07:16:01)
[GCC 4.9.2] on linux
Type "copyright", "credits" or "license()" for more information.
>>> import numpy as np
>>> lst=[10,20,30,40,50]
>>> np.array(lst,dtype='float64')
array([ 10., 20., 30., 40., 50.])
>>>
```
                                                                    Ln: 8 Col: 4

FIGURE 3.29 Python Command Code to Convert a List of Integers to an Array of Double Precision Floating Point Values of Type float64.

Here we observe that a list of integers is converted into an array of double-precision floating-point values of type float64.

3.18.2 Creating Arrays with NumPy

To create a single dimensional array of 20 elements filled with 0s, we use the following command np.zeros(20, dtype′int64′). This is visualized in Figure 3.30.

```
File  Edit  Shell  Debug  Options  Windows  Help
Python 3.4.2 (default, Sep 26 2018, 07:16:01)
[GCC 4.9.2] on linux
Type "copyright", "credits" or "license()" for more information.
>>> import numpy as np
>>> np.zeros(20,dtype='int64')
array([0, 0, 0, 0, 0, 0, 0, 0, 0, 0, 0, 0, 0, 0, 0, 0, 0, 0, 0, 0], dtype=int64)
>>>
                                                                    Ln: 7 Col: 4
```

FIGURE 3.30   Python Command Code to Create a Single Dimensional Array of 20 Elements Filled with 0s.

Now let us create a single dimensional array with values filled from 0 to 9. We can accomplish this with the command np.arange(0,10,1). Here 0 is the starting element, 10 is the max range and 1 is the step function. This is illustrated in Figure 3.31.

```
File  Edit  Shell  Debug  Options  Windows  Help
Python 3.4.2 (default, Sep 26 2018, 07:16:01)
[GCC 4.9.2] on linux
Type "copyright", "credits" or "license()" for more information.
>>> import numpy as np
>>> np.arange(0,10,1)
array([0, 1, 2, 3, 4, 5, 6, 7, 8, 9])
>>>
                                                                    Ln: 7 Col: 4
```

FIGURE 3.31   Python Command Code to Create a Single Dimensional Array with Values Filled from 0 to 9.

We have not specified dtype, and it generates values of integer types.

To generate floating-point values, we may as well specify dtype = 'float64'. Thus, we get the following

```
File  Edit  Shell  Debug  Options  Windows  Help
Python 3.4.2 (default, Sep 26 2018, 07:16:01)
[GCC 4.9.2] on linux
Type "copyright", "credits" or "license()" for more information.
>>> import numpy as np
>>> np.arange(0,10,1,dtype='float64')
array([ 0.,  1.,  2.,  3.,  4.,  5.,  6.,  7.,  8.,  9.])
>>>
                                                                    Ln: 7 Col: 4
```

FIGURE 3.32   Python Command Code to Create a Single Dimensional Array with Floating Point Values Filled from 0 to 9.

To generate random floating-point values between 0 and 4 and for a 2-Dimensional matrix of the range 4 x 4, we can use the following command.

$$np.random.random((4,4)) * 4 + 0$$

The random.random() command returns floating-point values between 0 to 1. However, as we have defined that we want values between 0 and 4, our lower bound remains the same (i.e., 0). To get the upper bound we need to multiply by 4, the value required in our case. Also, the lower bound can be specified by adding the same, which can be safely ignored in our case as the lower bound is 0. Thus, the command to generate random floating-point values between 0 and 4 and for a 2-dimensional matrix of the range 4 x 4 can be rewritten as

$$np.random.random((4,4)) * 4$$

Both of these commands accomplish our requirement. This is illustrated in Figure 3.33.

```
File  Edit  Shell  Debug  Options  Windows  Help
Python 3.4.2 (default, Sep 26 2018, 07:16:01)
[GCC 4.9.2] on linux
Type "copyright", "credits" or "license()" for more information.
>>> import numpy as np
>>> np.random.random((4,4))*4+0
array([[ 1.11502942,   3.05556544,   3.2371537 ,   3.37282423],
       [ 0.95828418,   2.46652166,   3.90770709,   0.62666558],
       [ 0.71685197,   2.49734463,   0.23147238,   0.85057937],
       [ 1.04934757,   3.3501376 ,   0.56577346,   3.52416782]])
>>> np.random.random((4,4))*4
array([[ 1.10756665,   3.31185856,   3.47170636,   3.37581423],
       [ 2.81952911,   3.62720586,   0.54124163,   1.60030299],
       [ 1.60699322,   2.97574266,   3.46282441,   0.81276109],
       [ 3.94777875,   3.67569579,   2.06327817,   1.55804204]])
>>>
                                                          Ln: 15 Col: 4
```

FIGURE 3.33   Python Command Code to Create 2-dimensional 4 x 4 Matrix of Random Floating Point Values.

Suppose we want to generate a 2-dimensional array of random values in the range 2 to 4. We can use the following command

$$np.random.random((4,4)) * 4 + 2$$

```
File  Edit  Shell  Debug  Options  Windows  Help
Python 3.4.2 (default, Sep 26 2018, 07:16:01)
[GCC 4.9.2] on linux
Type "copyright", "credits" or "license()" for more information.
>>> import numpy as np
>>> np.random.random((4,4))*4+2
array([[ 4.34949209,  5.63659194,  3.66355355,  3.81892803],
       [ 3.61461223,  4.36276996,  3.47578292,  2.45625841],
       [ 2.10801162,  4.23268329,  4.6262672 ,  2.08349686],
       [ 5.34018257,  3.05800764,  5.34124995,  4.28341959]])
>>>
                                                        Ln: 10 Col: 4
```

FIGURE 3.34   Python Command Code to Create 2-dimensional 4 x 4 Matrix of Random Floating Point Values between 0 and 4.

Here we observe that adding 2 provides us with the lower bound.

Now suppose we want to create a 2-dimensional array of dimensions 3 x 3 filled with 1s of Integer64 type; we need to use the following command

$$np.ones((3,3),\ dtype = 'int64')$$

This is illustrated as in Figure 3.35.

```
File  Edit  Shell  Debug  Options  Windows  Help
Python 3.4.2 (default, Sep 26 2018, 07:16:01)
[GCC 4.9.2] on linux
Type "copyright", "credits" or "license()" for more information.
>>> import numpy as np
>>> np.ones((3,3),dtype='int64')
array([[1, 1, 1],
       [1, 1, 1],
       [1, 1, 1]], dtype=int64)
>>>
                                                        Ln: 9 Col: 4
```

FIGURE 3.35   Python Command Code to Create a 2-dimensional Array of Dimensions 3 x 3 Filled with 1s of Integer64 type.

3.18.3 Basic NumPy Operations

- Array Attributes: In most data-processing applications, the developers need to be aware of the array attributes. The attributes and their descriptions are illustrated in Table 3.5.

TABLE 3.5   NumPy Array Attributes

Attribute	Description
ndim	Specifies the number of dimensions
shape	Specifies the size of each dimension
size	Specifies the total size of the array
dtype	Specifies the datatype of the array elements

Consider a 2-dimensional array with dimensions 3 x 3 as follows

$$1 \quad 2 \quad 3$$
$$4 \quad 5 \quad 6$$
$$7 \quad 8 \quad 9$$

Now using NumPy we create the above array and print its attributes.

```
File  Edit  Shell  Debug  Options  Windows  Help
Python 3.4.2 (default, Sep 26 2018, 07:16:01)
[GCC 4.9.2] on linux
Type "copyright", "credits" or "license()" for more information.
>>> import numpy as np
>>> a=np.arange(1,10,1).reshape(3,3)
>>> print(a)
[[1 2 3]
 [4 5 6]
 [7 8 9]]
>>> print("No of dimensions of a: ",a.ndim)
No of dimensions of a:  2
>>> print("Size of dimension of a: ",a.shape)
Size of dimension of a:  (3, 3)
>>> print("Total size of array a: ",a.size)
Total size of array a:  9
>>> print("Datatype of elements of a: ",a.dtype)
Datatype of elements of a:  int32
>>>
                                                        Ln: 18 Col: 4
```

FIGURE 3.36 Python Command Code to Create a 2-Dimensional Array of Dimensions 3 X 3 and Print Its Attributes.

The method reshape() is used to build a matrix of 3 x 3 with elements 1 to 9. The method reshape() will be discussed more elaborately in the following sections.

- **Array indexing**

The array index in Python starts from 0. Thus if we have to get the 5th element of the array we need to say array_name[4]. This is illustrated in the Figure 3.37.

```
File  Edit  Shell  Debug  Options  Windows  Help
Python 3.4.2 (default, Sep 26 2018, 07:16:01)
[GCC 4.9.2] on linux
Type "copyright", "credits" or "license()" for more information.
>>> import numpy as np
>>> a=np.array([10,20,30,40,50])
>>> print(a)
[10 20 30 40 50]
>>> print(a[4])
50
>>>
                                                          Ln: 10 Col: 4
```

FIGURE 3.37   Python Command Code to Access Array Elements.

To access a multi-dimensional array we need to have a comma separated tuple of indices to access the array. Example array_name[2][1] will return the value of the element at the third row and second column. This is illustrated with the example in Figure 3.38.

```
File  Edit  Shell  Debug  Options  Windows  Help
Python 3.4.2 (default, Sep 26 2018, 07:16:01)
[GCC 4.9.2] on linux
Type "copyright", "credits" or "license()" for more information.
>>> import numpy as np
>>> a=np.array([[10,20,30,40],
                [50,60,70,80],
                [90,100,110,120]])
>>> print(a)
[[ 10   20   30   40]
 [ 50   60   70   80]
 [ 90  100  110  120]]
>>> print(a[2][1])
100
>>>
                                                          Ln: 14 Col: 4
```

FIGURE 3.38   Python Command Code to Access Multi-dimensional Array Elements.

- **Working with subarrays.**

To get a subarray from an array we use the slicing operations similar to Python lists.

The syntax is array_name[intial_value, final_value, step_value]

1-Dimensional array

Let us consider a 1-Dimensional array with values 0, 1, 2, 3, 4, 5, 6.

Index	0	1	2	3	4	5	6
Values	0	1	2	3	4	5	6

To get the first three values, we need to execute the statement a [:3]. This says values that are at index 0, index 1 and index 2. To get the last three values we need to execute the Python statement a[4:]. This says all values that are after index 4. This is illustrated as in Figure 3.39.

```
File Edit Shell Debug Options Windows Help
Python 3.4.2 (default, Sep 26 2018, 07:16:01)
[GCC 4.9.2] on linux
Type "copyright", "credits" or "license()" for more information.
>>> import numpy as np
>>> a=np.arange(0,7,1)
>>> print(a)
[0 1 2 3 4 5 6]
>>> print("The first three values of a are :",a[:3])
The first three values of a are : [0 1 2]
>>> print("The last three values of a are :",a[4:1])
The last three values of a are : []
>>> print("The middle values of the array a are: ",a[2:5])
The middle values of the array a are:  [2 3 4]
>>>
                                                          Ln: 14 Col: 4
```

FIGURE 3.39   Python Command Code to Get Subarray from Array.

In Figure 3.39 we see that to get the middle values of an array a we splice it with the following range a[2:5] (i.e., all value greater than index 2 means starting from value 3, and up to index 5 means up to value 4).

2-dimensional array

In case of 2-dimensional arrays, the multiple splices are separated by commas.

For example, if we have a 2-D array of dimensions 3 x 3 as follows

$$1 \quad 2 \quad 3$$
$$4 \quad 5 \quad 6$$
$$7 \quad 8 \quad 9$$

Now using NumPy, we want to get the values of the single column we need to execute the following statements

$$2$$
$$5$$
$$8$$

$$a[: 3, 1 : 2]$$

This is illustrated in Figure 3.40.

```
File Edit Shell Debug Options Windows Help
Python 3.4.2 (default, Sep 26 2018, 07:16:01)
[GCC 4.9.2] on linux
Type "copyright", "credits" or "license()" for more information.
>>> import numpy as np
>>> a=np.arange(1,10,1).reshape(3,3)
>>> print(a)
[[1 2 3]
 [4 5 6]
 [7 8 9]]
>>> print("Required Column is: ",a[:3,1:2])
Required Column is:  [[2]
 [5]
 [8]]
>>>
                                                    Ln: 14 Col: 4
```

FIGURE 3.40   Python Command Code to Get Subarray from 2-D Array.

Thus, we fetch 3 rows from array **a** for columns that start at index 1 and are less than index 2 (i.e., the entire column at index 1).

Note: The subarrays created by NumPy are treated as views. Thus, if the subarray elements are modified, they are reflected back in the original array. This is illustrated in Figure 3.41.

```
File Edit Shell Debug Options Windows Help
Python 3.4.2 (default, Sep 26 2018, 07:16:01)
[GCC 4.9.2] on linux
Type "copyright", "credits" or "license()" for more information.
>>> import numpy as np
>>> a=np.arange(1,10,1).reshape(3,3)
>>> print(a)
[[1 2 3]
 [4 5 6]
 [7 8 9]]
>>> a[1,2]=10
>>> print(a)
[[ 1  2  3]
 [ 4  5 10]
 [ 7  8  9]]
>>>
                                                          Ln: 15 Col: 4
```

FIGURE 3.41   Python Command Code to Get Subarray from 2-D Array.

Here we modify 2 row 3rd element and assign it with a value 10. This is reflected back in the array **a** when we print out the same.

- **Copying an array**

We can make another copy of an array with the copy() function. This is illustrated in Figure 3.42.

```
File Edit Shell Debug Options Windows Help
Python 3.4.2 (default, Sep 26 2018, 07:16:01)
[GCC 4.9.2] on linux
Type "copyright", "credits" or "license()" for more information.
>>> import numpy as np
>>> a=np.arange(1,10,1).reshape(3,3)
>>> print(a)
[[1 2 3]
 [4 5 6]
 [7 8 9]]
>>> b=a[0:,:3].copy()
>>> print(b)
[[1 2 3]
 [4 5 6]
 [7 8 9]]
>>>
                                                          Ln: 15 Col: 4
```

FIGURE 3.42   Python Command Code to Copy an Array.

- **Array reshaping**

At times, we need to change the shape of an array (i.e., from a row-vector to a column-vector). This is illustrated in the example shown in Figure 3.43.

```
File  Edit  Shell  Debug  Options  Windows  Help
Python 3.4.2 (default, Sep 26 2018, 07:16:01)
[GCC 4.9.2] on linux
Type "copyright", "credits" or "license()" for more information.
>>> import numpy as np
>>> a=np.arange(1,9,1).reshape(1,8)
>>> print(a)
[[1 2 3 4 5 6 7 8]]
>>> a.reshape(8,1)
array([[1],
       [2],
       [3],
       [4],
       [5],
       [6],
       [7],
       [8]])
>>>
                                                              Ln: 17 Col: 4
```

FIGURE 3.43   Python Command Code to Change the Shape of an Array.

- **Array Concatenation**

It is possible to club two arrays into a single one through the concatenation process. The first routine we consider is np.concatenate(). This is illustrated in Figure 3.44.

Axis in NumPy are with respect to multi-dimensional arrays. For example, a 2-dimensional array has two axes. If axis=0, that means a straight axis running downwards across the rows. Alternatively, if axis=1, that means a straight axis running horizontally across the columns.

Let us consider the concatenation of two 1-dimensional arrays. This is illustrated in Figure 3.44.

```
File  Edit  Shell  Debug  Options  Windows  Help
Python 3.4.2 (default, Sep 26 2018, 07:16:01)
[GCC 4.9.2] on linux
Type "copyright", "credits" or "license()" for more information.
>>> import numpy as np
>>> a=np.array([10,20,30])
>>> b=np.array([40,50,60])
>>> print(a)
[10 20 30]
>>> print(b)
[40 50 60]
>>> c=np.concatenate([a,b])
>>> print(c)
[10 20 30 40 50 60]
>>>
                                                              Ln: 14 Col: 4
```

FIGURE 3.44   Python Command Code to Concatenate Two 1-dimensional Arrays.

The concatenation operation of multi-dimensional arrays is based on the axis. If the axis=0 it means the concatenation will be done vertically, and if the axis=1, it means the concatenation will be done horizontally. This is illustrated with the examples in Figures 3.45 and 3.46.

```
File  Edit  Shell  Debug  Options  Windows  Help
Python 3.4.2 (default, Sep 26 2018, 07:16:01)
[GCC 4.9.2] on linux
Type "copyright", "credits" or "license()" for more information.
>>> import numpy as np
>>> a=np.array([[10,20,30],
                [40,50,60],
                [70,80,90]])
>>> b=np.array([[2,2,2],
                [2,2,2],
                [2,2,2]])
>>> c=np.concatenate([a,b],axis=0)
>>> print(a)
[[10 20 30]
 [40 50 60]
 [70 80 90]]
>>> print(b)
[[2 2 2]
 [2 2 2]
 [2 2 2]]
>>> print("Vertical Concatenation")
Vertical Concatenation
>>> print(c)
[[10 20 30]
 [40 50 60]
 [70 80 90]
 [ 2  2  2]
 [ 2  2  2]
 [ 2  2  2]]
>>>
                                                    Ln: 29 Col: 4
```

FIGURE 3.45 Python Command Code to Concatenate Multi-dimensional Array Vertically.

```
File  Edit  Shell  Debug  Options  Windows  Help
Python 3.4.2 (default, Sep 26 2018, 07:16:01)
[GCC 4.9.2] on linux
Type "copyright", "credits" or "license()" for more information.
>>> import numpy as np
>>> a=np.array([[10,20,30],
                [40,50,60],
                [70,80,90]])
>>> b=np.array([[2,2,2],
                [2,2,2],
                [2,2,2]])
>>> c=np.concatenate([a,b],axis=1)
>>> print(a)
[[10 20 30]
 [40 50 60]
 [70 80 90]]
>>> print(b)
[[2 2 2]
 [2 2 2]
 [2 2 2]]
>>> print("Horizontal Concatenation")
Horizontal Concatenation
>>> print(c)
[[10 20 30  2  2  2]
 [40 50 60  2  2  2]
 [70 80 90  2  2  2]]
>>>
                                                    Ln: 26 Col: 4
```

FIGURE 3.46 Python Command Code to Concatenate Multi-dimensional Array Horizontally.

If the arrays are of different dimensions and you want to concatenate them, then you can use vstack() vertical stack or hstack() horizontal stack routines. This is illustrated in the example below.

```
File  Edit  Shell  Debug  Options  Windows  Help
Python 3.4.2 (default, Sep 26 2018, 07:16:01)
[GCC 4.9.2] on linux
Type "copyright", "credits" or "license()" for more information.
>>> import numpy as np
>>> a=np.array([10,20,30])
>>> b=np.array([[40,50,60],
                [70,80,90]])
>>> c=np.array([10,20]).reshape(-1,1)
>>> d=np.vstack([a,b])
>>> e=np.hstack([b,c])
>>> print(a)
[10 20 30]
>>> print(b)
[[40 50 60]
 [70 80 90]]
>>> print(c)
[[10]
 [20]]
>>> print(d)
[[10 20 30]
 [40 50 60]
 [70 80 90]]
>>> print(e)
[[40 50 60 10]
 [70 80 90 20]]
>>>
                                                          Ln: 26 Col: 4
```

FIGURE 3.47 Python Command Code to Concatenate Arrays of Different Dimensions.

- **Splitting Arrays**

Sometimes we need to split an array into different arrays. This is accomplished with the split() function. If the split of the array is going to be into arrays of unequal sizes, then you need to give the split points. This is illustrated in Figure 3.48.

```
File  Edit  Shell  Debug  Options  Windows  Help
Python 3.4.2 (default, Sep 26 2018, 07:16:01)
[GCC 4.9.2] on linux
Type "copyright", "credits" or "license()" for more information.
>>> import numpy as np
>>> a=np.array([10,20,30,40,50,60,70,80,90,100])
>>> a1,a2,a3=np.split(a,[3,7])
>>> print(a1)
[10 20 30]
>>> print(a2)
[40 50 60 70]
>>> print(a3)
[ 80  90 100]
>>>
                                                          Ln: 13 Col: 4
```

FIGURE 3.48 Python Command Code to Split Arrays of Unequal Sizes.

$$a1, a2, a3 = np.split(a, [3, 7])$$

Here the split for the first array is 0 to 2, for the second array 3 to 6 and for the third array it is 7 to 9. This we have accomplished with the split points[3,7].

However, there is another way of splitting an array to unequal sizes. This is accomplished with the routine array_split() and is illustrated in Figure 3.49.

```
File  Edit  Shell  Debug  Options  Windows  Help
Python 3.4.2 (default, Sep 26 2018, 07:16:01)
[GCC 4.9.2] on linux
Type "copyright", "credits" or "license()" for more information.
>>> import numpy as np
>>> a=np.array([10,20,30,40,50,60,70,80,90,100])
>>> a1,a2,a3=np.array_split(a,3)
>>> print(a1)
[10 20 30 40]
>>> print(a2)
[50 60 70]
>>> print(a3)
[ 80  90 100]
>>>
                                                    Ln: 13 Col: 4
```

FIGURE 3.49 Python Command Code to Split Arrays of Unequal Sizes with Array_Split().

3.19 PANDAS INTRODUCTION

Pandas is one of the essential Python libraries you need to study as a productive data scientist. In brief, Pandas builds upon the capabilities of NumPy arrays into labeled rows and columns.

Pandas can be visualized as the sum of NumPy array capabilities with the power of spreadsheets and relational databases.

A small subset of Pandas applications includes

- Converting a NumPy array, Python list or dictionary into a Pandas dataframe object.

- Opening a locally stored csv file.

- Helping to open a remote csv file through a URL.

3.19.1 Exploring Pandas

To check whether Pandas has been installed properly, you can type the command illustrated in Figure 3.50.

```
File  Edit  Shell  Debug  Options  Windows  Help
Python 3.4.2 (default, Sep 26 2018, 07:16:01)
[GCC 4.9.2] on linux
Type "copyright", "credits" or "license()" for more information.
>>> import pandas as pd
>>>
                                                           Ln: 5 Col: 4
```

FIGURE 3.50   Python Command Code to Check Whether Pandas Is Installed Properly.

If you get the interpreter prompt without any errors, that means Pandas has been installed properly.

The two preliminary data structures of Pandas you need to study are Series and DataFrame.

```
File  Edit  Shell  Debug  Options  Windows  Help
Python 3.4.2 (default, Sep 26 2018, 07:16:01)
[GCC 4.9.2] on linux
Type "copyright", "credits" or "license()" for more information.
>>> import pandas as pd
>>> pdata=pd.Series([10,20,30,40,50])
>>> pdata
0    10
1    20
2    30
3    40
4    50
dtype: int64
>>>
                                                           Ln: 13 Col: 4
```

FIGURE 3.51   Python Command Code to Demonstrate Use of Pandas Series Object.

In Pandas official documentation, a Series is described as a homogeneously typed structure. Let us consider the example illustrated in Figure 3.52.

```
File  Edit  Shell  Debug  Options  Windows  Help
Python 3.4.2 (default, Sep 26 2018, 07:16:01)
[GCC 4.9.2] on linux
Type "copyright", "credits" or "license()" for more information.
>>> import pandas as pd
>>> pdata=pd.Series([10,20,30,40,'a'])
>>> pdata
0    10
1    20
2    30
3    40
4     a
dtype: object
>>>

                                                          Ln: 13 Col: 4
```

FIGURE 3.52 Python Command Code to Demonstrate Use of Pandas Series Object for Upcast.

Here we observe that the Series object allowed us to insert a string 'a'. Thus, the presence of int and string has resulted in an upcast of the type object. If the array contains integers and floats, the array type will be upcasted to float. This is visualized with the help of the example as illustrated in Figure 3.53.

```
File  Edit  Shell  Debug  Options  Windows  Help
Python 3.4.2 (default, Sep 26 2018, 07:16:01)
[GCC 4.9.2] on linux
Type "copyright", "credits" or "license()" for more information.
>>> import pandas as pd
>>> pdata=pd.Series([10,20,30,40,1.2])
>>> pdata
0    10.0
1    20.0
2    30.0
3    40.0
4     1.2
dtype: float64
>>>

                                                          Ln: 13 Col: 4
```

FIGURE 3.53 Python Command Code to Demonstrate Use of Pandas Series Object for Upcast from Integers to Floats.

Here we observe that the series object contained integers and floats and has been upcasted to floats.

Note: Although the Series object will permit non-homogeneous elements, certain Pandas functions may not work correctly.

Since for the above series object we did not specify an index, it by default took an index from 0 to N-1 where N is the number of elements in the Series object.

Subarray can be obtained by splicing the Series object in Pandas like NumPy. This is illustrated in Figure 3.54.

```
File  Edit  Shell  Debug  Options  Windows  Help
Python 3.4.2 (default, Sep 26 2018, 07:16:01)
[GCC 4.9.2] on linux
Type "copyright", "credits" or "license()" for more information.
>>> import pandas as pd
>>> pdata=pd.Series([10,20,30,40,50])
>>> pdata
0    10
1    20
2    30
3    40
4    50
dtype: int64
>>> pdata[0:3]
0    10
1    20
2    30
dtype: int64
>>> pdata[:]
0    10
1    20
2    30
3    40
4    50
dtype: int64
>>>
                                              Ln: 25 Col: 4
```

FIGURE 3.54   Python Command Code to Generate Sub-array Using Splicing of Series Object.

In the case of a series object in Pandas, we can access index using strings and not restrict ourselves to integers like NumPy. This is illustrated in the example in Figure 3.55.

```
File Edit Shell Debug Options Windows Help
Python 3.4.2 (default, Sep 26 2018, 07:16:01)
[GCC 4.9.2] on linux
Type "copyright", "credits" or "license()" for more information.
>>> import pandas as pd
>>> pdata=pd.Series([10,20,30,40,50],index=['p','q','r','s','t'])
>>> pdata
p    10
q    20
r    30
s    40
t    50
dtype: int64
>>> pdata['r']
30
>>> pdata['s']
40
>>> pdata['q':'t']
q    20
r    30
s    40
t    50
dtype: int64
>>>
                                                          Ln: 23 Col: 4
```

FIGURE 3.55   Python Command Code to Acess Series Object Index Using Strings.

The Pandas Series object could be visualized as a Python dictionary. Here the corresponding keys and their values are mapped together. This is illustrated in Figure 3.56.

```
File Edit Shell Debug Options Windows Help
Python 3.4.2 (default, Sep 26 2018, 07:16:01)
[GCC 4.9.2] on linux
Type "copyright", "credits" or "license()" for more information.
>>> import pandas as pd
>>> dict1={'a':1,'b':2,'c':3,'d':4,'e':5}
>>> pdata=pd.Series(dict1)
>>> pdata
a    1
b    2
c    3
d    4
e    5
dtype: int64
>>> pdata['a']
1
>>>
                                                          Ln: 16 Col: 4
```

FIGURE 3.56   Python Command Code to Implement Series Object as Dictionary.

Here, the indices are the keys of the dictionary in the sorted form.

3.19.2 DataFrame Object

A DataFrame is a tabular structure like a spreadsheet in which each column represents different values. It can also be visualized as a collection of 1-dimensional Series objects.

Thus a DataFrame can be thought of as a page in a spreadsheet. This is illustrated in Table 3.4.

Let us try to depict a state, its capital and the capital's population.

TABLE 3.4   Table of a state, capital and population

State	Capital	Population
Alabama	Montgomery	198,232
Florida	Tallahassee	193,078
Louisiana	Baton Rouge	226,505
Massachusetts	Boston	687,584
Virginia	Richmond	230,254

```
File Edit Shell Debug Options Windows Help
Python 3.4.2 (default, Sep 26 2018, 07:16:01)
[GCC 4.9.2] on linux
Type "copyright", "credits" or "license()" for more information.
>>> import pandas as pd
>>> dict_info={
        'state':["Alabama","Florida","Louisiana","Massachusetts","Virginia"],
        'capital':["Montgomery","Tallahassee","Baton Rouge","Boston","Richmond"],
        'population':[198232,193078,226505,687584,230254]
        }
>>> dataf=pd.DataFrame(dict_info)
>>> dataf
        capital  population          state
0   Montgomery      198232        Alabama
1  Tallahassee      193078        Florida
2  Baton Rouge      226505      Louisiana
3       Boston      687584  Massachusetts
4     Richmond      230254       Virginia
>>>
                                                            Ln: 18 Col: 4
```

FIGURE 3.57   Python Command Code to Demonstrate Dataframe as a Tabular Structure.

As we have not specified the row indexes, it has taken the index values from 0 to 4. We can access the DataFrame object by specifying the column name or by getting the data from a specific row.

Example: dataf['state']

To get specific row data we can use the following

dataf.ix[1]

Here ix stands for indexing field. This is illustrated in Figure 3.58.

```
File  Edit  Shell  Debug  Options  Windows  Help
Python 3.4.2 (default, Sep 26 2018, 07:16:01)
[GCC 4.9.2] on linux
Type "copyright", "credits" or "license()" for more information.
>>> import pandas as pd
>>> dict_info={
        'state':["Alabama","Florida","Louisiana","Massachusetts","Virginia"],
        'capital':["Montgomery","Tallahassee","Baton Rouge","Boston","Richmond"],
        'population':[198232,193078,226505,687584,230254]
        }
>>> dataf=pd.DataFrame(dict_info)
>>> dataf
        capital  population           state
0     Montgomery      198232         Alabama
1    Tallahassee      193078         Florida
2    Baton Rouge      226505       Louisiana
3         Boston      687584   Massachusetts
4       Richmond      230254        Virginia
>>> dataf['state']
0          Alabama
1          Florida
2        Louisiana
3    Massachusetts
4         Virginia
Name: state, dtype: object
>>> dataf.ix[1]
capital        Tallahassee
population          193078
state              Florida
Name: 1, dtype: object
>>>
                                                              Ln: 30 Col: 4
```

FIGURE 3.58   Python Command Code to Access Dataframe Object.

The datatype of the columns of a DataFrame object are of the same type. We can get the data types of all columns by specifying

dataframeobject.dtypes

We can also get the datatype of a specific column by writing

dataframeobject['column_name'].dtype

```
File Edit Shell Debug Options Windows Help
Python 3.4.2 (default, Sep 26 2018, 07:16:01)
[GCC 4.9.2] on linux
Type "copyright", "credits" or "license()" for more information.
>>> import pandas as pd
>>> dict_info={
        'state':["Alabama","Florida","Louisiana","Massachusetts","Virginia"],
        'capital':["Montgomery","Tallahassee","Baton Rouge","Boston","Richmond"],
        'population':[198232,193078,226505,687584,230254]
        }
>>> dataf=pd.DataFrame(dict_info)
>>> dataf.dtypes
capital        object
population      int64
state          object
dtype: object
>>> dataf['state'].dtype
dtype('O')
>>>
                                                          Ln: 18 Col: 4
```

FIGURE 3.59   Python Command Code to Access Dataframe Object.

As a Pandas DataFrame object contains many records, it is sometime useful to check a limited number of sample records from the top or the bottom. Pandas provides functions like head() and tail() to accomplish the same.

This is illustrated with the in Figure 3.60.

```
File Edit Shell Debug Options Windows Help
Python 3.4.2 (default, Sep 26 2018, 07:16:01)
[GCC 4.9.2] on linux
Type "copyright", "credits" or "license()" for more information.
>>> import pandas as pd
>>> dict_info={
        'state':["Alabama","Florida","Louisiana","Massachusetts","Virginia"],
        'capital':["Montgomery","Tallahassee","Baton Rouge","Boston","Richmond"],
        'population':[198232,193078,226505,687584,230254]
        }
>>> dataf=pd.DataFrame(dict_info)
>>> dataf
        capital  population           state
0    Montgomery      198232         Alabama
1   Tallahassee      193078         Florida
2   Baton Rouge      226505       Louisiana
3        Boston      687584   Massachusetts
4      Richmond      230254        Virginia
>>> dataf.head(2)
        capital  population    state
0    Montgomery      198232  Alabama
1   Tallahassee      193078  Florida
>>> dataf.tail(2)
      capital  population           state
3      Boston      687584   Massachusetts
4    Richmond      230254        Virginia
>>>
                                                          Ln: 26 Col: 4
```

FIGURE 3.60   Python Command Code to Create Dataframe Object Dict_Info.

To view the available indexes and column names, we can use Pandas capabilities like

dataobjectname.index

dataobjectname.columns

This is illustrated in Figure 3.61.

```
File Edit Shell Debug Options Windows Help
Python 3.4.2 (default, Sep 26 2018, 07:16:01)
[GCC 4.9.2] on linux
Type "copyright", "credits" or "license()" for more information.
>>> import pandas as pd
>>> dict_info={
        'state':["Alabhama","Florida","Louisiana","Massachusetts","Virginia"],
        'capital':["Montgomery","Tallahassee","Baton Rouge","Boston","Richmond"],
        'population':[198232,193078,226505,687584,230254]
        }
>>> dataf=pd.DataFrame(dict_info)
>>> dataf
        capital  population          state
0   Montgomery      198232       Alabhama
1  Tallahassee      193078        Florida
2  Baton Rouge      226505      Louisiana
3       Boston      687584  Massachusetts
4     Richmond      230254       Virginia
>>> dataf.index
Int64Index([0, 1, 2, 3, 4], dtype='int64')
>>> dataf.columns
Index(['capital', 'population', 'state'], dtype='object')
>>>
                                                            Ln: 22 Col: 4
```

FIGURE 3.61   Python Command Code to View Available Indexes and Column Names in a Dataframe Object dict_info.

3.19.2.1 DataFrame Column Functions

There are times when you would want to extract some column-level functions; under such circumstances, you could make use of Column Functions

mean(): the mean of the specified column values

unique(): the unique values of a column

sum(): sum of the values of the specified column

max(): highest value of the specified column

min(): lowest value of the specified column

idxmin(): the index of the lowest value

idxmax(): the index of the highest value

count(): the number of non-null values in a specified column

describe(): the statistical summary

This is illustrated in Figure 3.62.

```
File Edit Shell Debug Options Windows Help
Python 3.4.2 (default, Sep 26 2018, 07:16:01)
[GCC 4.9.2] on linux
Type "copyright", "credits" or "license()" for more information.
>>> import pandas as pd
>>> dict_info={
        'state':["Alabhama","Florida","Louisiana","Massachusetts","Virginia"],
        'capital':["Montgomery","Tallahassee","Baton Rouge","Boston","Richmond"],
        'population':[198232,193078,226505,687584,230254],
        'mortality_rate':[9.2,6.66,8.7,6.69,7.15]
        }
>>> dataf=pd.DataFrame(dict_info)
>>> dataf
        capital  mortality_rate  population          state
0    Montgomery            9.20      198232        Alabhama
1   Tallahassee            6.66      193078         Florida
2   Baton Rouge            8.70      226505       Louisiana
3        Boston            6.69      687584   Massachusetts
4      Richmond            7.15      230254        Virginia
>>> print("Least Mortality Rate: ",dataf.mortality_rate.min())
Least Mortality Rate:  6.66
>>> print("Highest Population: ",dataf.population.max())
Highest Population:  687584
>>> print("Average Mortality Rate: ",dataf.mortality_rate.sum()/dataf.mortality_rate.count())
Average Mortality Rate:  7.68
>>>
                                                                              Ln: 25 Col: 4
```

FIGURE 3.62   Python Command Code to View Available Indexes and Column Names in a Dataframe Object dict_info.

3.19.2.2 Pandas Functionalities for DataFrame Information

Pandas provides functionalities where we can extract information about the DataFrame like shape, columns and the index used.

The syntax is

dataframeobject.shape: the number of rows and columns in the Data-Frame object

dataframeobject.columns: the columns specified in the DataFrame object

Dataframeobject.index: details of the row index including the range

This is illustrated in Figure 3.63.

```
File Edit Shell Debug Options Windows Help
Python 3.4.2 (default, Sep 26 2018, 07:16:01)
[GCC 4.9.2] on linux
Type "copyright", "credits" or "license()" for more information.
>>> import pandas as pd
>>> dict_info={
        'state':["Alabhama","Florida","Louisiana","Massachusetts","Virginia"],
        'capital':["Montgomery","Tallahassee","Baton Rouge","Boston","Richmond"],
        'population':[198232,193078,226505,687584,230254],
        'mortality_rate':[9.2,6.66,8.7,6.69,7.15]
        }
>>> dataf=pd.DataFrame(dict_info)
>>> dataf
        capital  mortality_rate  population         state
0    Montgomery            9.20      198232       Alabhama
1   Tallahassee            6.66      193078        Florida
2   Baton Rouge            8.70      226505      Louisiana
3        Boston            6.69      687584  Massachusetts
4      Richmond            7.15      230254       Virginia
>>> dataf.shape
(5, 4)
>>> dataf.columns
Index(['capital', 'mortality_rate', 'population', 'state'], dtype='object')
>>> dataf.index
Int64Index([0, 1, 2, 3, 4], dtype='int64')
>>>
```
```
                                                            Ln: 25 Col: 4
```

FIGURE 3.63   Python Command Code to Demonstrate Column Level Functions.

3.19.2.3 Pandas Functions to Remove Rows and Columns in a DataFrame

Pandas provides the drop function to remove the rows and columns in a DataFrame object.

First, consider an example in which you want to drop specific rows from a DataFrame. As we have not specified row names, the values would be from 0 to N-1. Thus, if we want to drop row0 and row1, we execute the following statement:

dataframeobject.drop([0,1])

If we had to drop a column, we would specify

dataframeobject.drop('column_name',axis=1)

This is illustrated in Figure 3.64.

```
File Edit Shell Debug Options Windows Help
Python 3.4.2 (default, Sep 26 2018, 07:16:01)
[GCC 4.9.2] on linux
Type "copyright", "credits" or "license()" for more information.
>>> import pandas as pd
>>> dict_info={
         'state':["Alabhama","Florida","Louisiana","Massachusetts","Virginia"],
         'capital':["Montgomery","Tallahassee","Baton Rouge","Boston","Richmond"],
         'population':[198232,193078,226505,687584,230254],
         'mortality_rate':[9.2,6.66,8.7,6.69,7.15]
         }
>>> dataf=pd.DataFrame(dict_info)
>>> dataf
        capital  mortality_rate  population          state
0    Montgomery            9.20      198232       Alabhama
1   Tallahassee            6.66      193078        Florida
2   Baton Rouge            8.70      226505      Louisiana
3        Boston            6.69      687584  Massachusetts
4      Richmond            7.15      230254       Virginia
>>> dataf.drop([0,1])
        capital  mortality_rate  population          state
2   Baton Rouge            8.70      226505      Louisiana
3        Boston            6.69      687584  Massachusetts
4      Richmond            7.15      230254       Virginia
>>> dataf.drop('mortality_rate',axis=1)
        capital  population          state
0    Montgomery     198232       Alabhama
1   Tallahassee     193078        Florida
2   Baton Rouge     226505      Louisiana
3        Boston     687584  Massachusetts
4      Richmond     230254       Virginia
>>>
                                                        Ln: 31  Col: 4
```

FIGURE 3.64   Python Command Code to Demonstrate Dataframe Information.

3.19.2.4 Modifying a DataFrame

To modify a DataFrame by adding a column, we can execute the following statement

$$dataframeobject['column\_name'] = 0$$

This will create a specified column and initialize its values to 0.

If you want to change the column names of a DataFrame object, you can execute the following statement.

$$Dataframeobject ['column\_name1', 'column\_name2', 'column\_name3', 'column\_name4']$$

Thus, the DataFrameObjects columns will be changed as specified by column_name1, column_name2, column_name3 and column_name4.

This is illustrated in Figure 3.65 and Figure 3.66.

```
File  Edit  Shell  Debug  Options  Windows  Help
Python 3.4.2 (default, Sep 26 2018, 07:16:01)
[GCC 4.9.2] on linux
Type "copyright", "credits" or "license()" for more information.
>>> import pandas as pd
>>> dict_info={
        'state':["Alabhama","Florida","Louisiana","Massachusetts","Virginia"],
        'capital':["Montgomery","Tallahassee","Baton Rouge","Boston","Richmond"],
        'population':[198232,193078,226505,687584,230254],
        'mortality_rate':[9.2,6.66,8.7,6.69,7.15]
        }
>>> dataf=pd.DataFrame(dict_info)
>>> dataf
      capital  mortality_rate  population         state
0  Montgomery            9.20      198232      Alabhama
1  Tallahassee           6.66      193078       Florida
2  Baton Rouge           8.70      226505     Louisiana
3      Boston            6.69      687584  Massachusetts
4    Richmond            7.15      230254      Virginia
>>> dataf['birth_rate']=0
>>> dataf
      capital  mortality_rate  population         state  birth_rate
0  Montgomery            9.20      198232      Alabhama           0
1  Tallahassee           6.66      193078       Florida           0
2  Baton Rouge           8.70      226505     Louisiana           0
3      Boston            6.69      687584  Massachusetts           0
4    Richmond            7.15      230254      Virginia           0
>>>
                                                              Ln: 27 Col: 4
```

FIGURE 3.65 Python Command Code to Modify DataFrame Information by Adding a Column.

```
File  Edit  Shell  Debug  Options  Windows  Help
Python 3.4.2 (default, Sep 26 2018, 07:16:01)
[GCC 4.9.2] on linux
Type "copyright", "credits" or "license()" for more information.
>>> import pandas as pd
>>> dict_info={
        'state':["Alabhama","Florida","Louisiana","Massachusetts","Virginia"],
        'capital':["Montgomery","Tallahassee","Baton Rouge","Boston","Richmond"],
        'population':[198232,193078,226505,687584,230254],
        'mortality_rate':[9.2,6.66,8.7,6.69,7.15]
        }
>>> dataf=pd.DataFrame(dict_info)
>>> dataf
      capital  mortality_rate  population         state
0  Montgomery            9.20      198232      Alabhama
1  Tallahassee           6.66      193078       Florida
2  Baton Rouge           8.70      226505     Louisiana
3      Boston            6.69      687584  Massachusetts
4    Richmond            7.15      230254      Virginia
>>> dataf.columns=['us_state','us_capital','us_population','us_mortality_rate']
>>> dataf
     us_state  us_capital  us_population  us_mortality_rate
0  Montgomery        9.20         198232           Alabhama
1  Tallahassee       6.66         193078            Florida
2  Baton Rouge       8.70         226505          Louisiana
3      Boston        6.69         687584      Massachusetts
4    Richmond        7.15         230254           Virginia
>>>
                                                              Ln: 27 Col: 4
```

FIGURE 3.66 Python Command Code to Modify DataFrame Information by Changing Column Names.

3.20 PANDAS FUNCTIONALITIES TO READ DATA FROM FILES

Let us first consider how to read data from a CSV file. CSV stands for comma separated values. It stores data that is delimited by commas; CSV files can be imported or exported to popular spreadsheets like Excel and officeorg.

Let us consider a simple CSV file called as **state.csv**

Step 1: In Python Shell say File -> NewFile.

Step 2: Paste your CSV content.

Step 3: Save the file (i.e., give **filename.csv** and choose type as **all files)**.

Note: Our created file is in the same folder in which Python can access files.

```
File  Edit  Format  Run  Options  Windows  Help
Montgomery,9.20,198232,Alabhama
Tallahassee,6.66,193078,Florida
Baton Rouge,8.70,226505,Louisiana
Boston,6.69,687584,Massachusetts
Richmond,7.15,230254,Virginia



                                                              Ln: 6 Col: 0
```

FIGURE 3.67   Snapshot of state.csv File.

To access this file using Pandas:

```
File  Edit  Shell  Debug  Options  Windows  Help
Python 3.4.2 (default, Sep 26 2018, 07:16:01)
[GCC 4.9.2] on linux
Type "copyright", "credits" or "license()" for more information.
>>> import pandas as pd
>>> pd.read_csv("state.csv",delimiter=',')
    Montgomery  9.20  198232       Alabhama
0   Tallahassee  6.66  193078        Florida
1   Baton Rouge  8.70  226505      Louisiana
2       Boston  6.69  687584  Massachusetts
3     Richmond  7.15  230254       Virginia
>>>


                                                              Ln: 11 Col: 4
```

FIGURE 3.68   Python Command Code to Access the csv File state.csv.

3.21 PANDAS MISSING DATA (DATA CLEANING)

Sometimes we come across missing values in a Pandas Series or DataFrame object. Pandas represents the missing value by NaN. It is useful to convert this NaN to the value 0 sometimes.

As an example, we have created a 1-dimensional array with a Series object as seen in Figure 3.69.

```
File Edit Shell Debug Options Windows Help
Python 3.4.2 (default, Sep 26 2018, 07:16:01)
[GCC 4.9.2] on linux
Type "copyright", "credits" or "license()" for more information.
>>> import pandas as pd
>>> import numpy as np
>>> parray=pd.Series([10,20,np.nan,30,40,np.nan])
>>> parray
0    10
1    20
2    NaN
3    30
4    40
5    NaN
dtype: float64
>>>
                                                              Ln: 15 Col: 4
```

FIGURE 3.69 Python Command Code to Create a 1-dimensional Array with a Series Object.

The first step would be to check the presence of missing data we can use the **isnull()** function. The usage of isnull() is illustrated in Figure 3.70.

```
File Edit Shell Debug Options Windows Help
Python 3.4.2 (default, Sep 26 2018, 07:16:01)
[GCC 4.9.2] on linux
Type "copyright", "credits" or "license()" for more information.
>>> import pandas as pd
>>> import numpy as np
>>> parray=pd.Series([10,20,np.nan,30,40,np.nan])
>>> parray
0    10
1    20
2    NaN
3    30
4    40
5    NaN
dtype: float64
>>> parray.isnull()
0    False
1    False
2     True
3    False
4    False
5     True
dtype: bool
>>>
                                                              Ln: 23 Col: 4
```

FIGURE 3.70 Python Command Code to Check the Presence of Missing Data in the Series Object.

Here we observe that row index 2 and row index 5 indicate True; that means there are values of NaN.

To remove these type of NaN values, we could use dropna() function, which drops rows or columns that have NaN values.

```
File  Edit  Shell  Debug  Options  Windows  Help
Python 3.4.2 (default, Sep 26 2018, 07:16:01)
[GCC 4.9.2] on linux
Type "copyright", "credits" or "license()" for more information.
>>> import pandas as pd
>>> import numpy as np
>>> pdata=pd.DataFrame([[10,20,30,np.nan],
                        ['a','b','c',np.nan],
                        [1.1,1.2,np.nan,1.3]])
>>> pdata
     0    1    2    3
0   10   20   30  NaN
1    a    b    c  NaN
2  1.1  1.2  NaN  1.3
>>> mdata=pdata.dropna(axis=1)
>>> mdata
     0    1
0   10   20
1    a    b
2  1.1  1.2
>>>
                                                          Ln: 20 Col: 4
```

FIGURE 3.71 Python Command Code to Remove NaN Values from a Data-Frame Object.

Here, column index 3 and column index 2 have NaN. Thus, when we delete column-wise, setting axis=1; only 2 columns are retained (i.e., column index 0 and column index 1, which do not have any NaN values).

The disadvantage of this method is that useful information associated with rows/columns having NaN values is lost.

To overcome this, we can replace NaN values with a value 0 or we can forward fill or backward fill the data.

```
File Edit Shell Debug Options Windows Help
Python 3.4.2 (default, Sep 26 2018, 07:16:01)
[GCC 4.9.2] on linux
Type "copyright", "credits" or "license()" for more information.
>>> import pandas as pd
>>> import numpy as np
>>> pdata=pd.DataFrame([[10,20,30,np.nan],
                        ['a','b','c',np.nan],
                        [1.1,1.2,np.nan,1.3]])
>>> pdata
     0    1    2    3
0   10   20   30  NaN
1    a    b    c  NaN
2  1.1  1.2  NaN  1.3
>>> pdata.fillna(0)
     0    1   2    3
0   10   20  30  0.0
1    a    b   c  0.0
2  1.1  1.2   0  1.3
>>>
                                                          Ln: 19 Col: 4
```

FIGURE 3.72   Python Command Code to Replace NaN Values with a Value 0.

The forward filling and backward filling of data are illustrated in Figure 3.73.

```
File Edit Shell Debug Options Windows Help
Python 3.4.2 (default, Sep 26 2018, 07:16:01)
[GCC 4.9.2] on linux
Type "copyright", "credits" or "license()" for more information.
>>> import pandas as pd
>>> import numpy as np
>>> pdata=pd.DataFrame([[10,20,30,np.nan],
                        ['a','b','c',np.nan],
                        [1.1,1.2,np.nan,1.3]])
>>> pdata
     0    1    2    3
0   10   20   30  NaN
1    a    b    c  NaN
2  1.1  1.2  NaN  1.3
>>> mdata=pdata.fillna(method='ffill')
>>> mdata
     0    1   2    3
0   10   20  30  NaN
1    a    b   c  NaN
2  1.1  1.2   c  1.3
>>> cdata=mdata.fillna(method='bfill')
>>> cdata
     0    1   2    3
0   10   20  30  1.3
1    a    b   c  1.3
2  1.1  1.2   c  1.3
>>>
                                                          Ln: 26 Col: 4
```

FIGURE 3.73   Python Command Code for Forward Filling and Backward Filling of Data.

3.22 SCIPY INTRODUCTION

SciPy is Python's library that helps scientists and engineers perform scientific computing. It provides supports toward the development of such applications as

- Optimization

- Integration

- Image Processing

- Statistics

3.22.1 Exploring SciPy

The first step is to check whether SciPy is installed properly.

```
File  Edit  Shell  Debug  Options  Windows  Help
Python 3.4.2 (default, Sep 26 2018, 07:16:01)
[GCC 4.9.2] on linux
Type "copyright", "credits" or "license()" for more information.
>>> import scipy
>>>
                                                        Ln: 5 Col: 4
```

FIGURE 3.74   Python Command Code to Check Whether SciPy Is Installed Properly.

If we get the command interpreter prompt without any error, which means SciPy has been installed properly.

3.22.2 Sparse Matrix

If a matrix contains a large number of zeros, we can call such matrix a sparse matrix.

Example

$$\begin{matrix} 1 & 0 & 0 \\ 0 & 0 & 3 \\ 0 & 0 & 0 \end{matrix}$$

In the above matrix there are 2 non-zero values, and the other 7 values are zero.

The formula to compute sparsity is

$$Number\ of\ zero\ elements/Total\ number\ of\ elements$$

Thus, the percentage of sparsity is (7/9)*100 = 77.78%, and the percentage of density is (2/9)*100 = 22.22%.

Common Sparse Row is often used to represent a sparse matrix in machine-learning applications. Here, three 1-dimensional matrices are used for non-zero values. This is illustrated with the example as illustrated in Figure 3.75 and Figure 3.76.

File Edit Format Run Options Windows Help

```
import numpy as np
from scipy.sparse import csr_matrix
a=np.array([[1,0,0],[0,0,3],[0,0,0]])
print(a,"\n")
b=csr_matrix(a)
print(b,"\n")
c=b.todense()
print(c,"\n")
```

Ln: 9 Col: 0

FIGURE 3.75   Python Program to Demonstrate a Sparse Matrix.

File Edit Shell Debug Options Windows Help

```
Python 3.4.2 (default, Sep 26 2018, 07:16:01)
[GCC 4.9.2] on linux
Type "copyright", "credits" or "license()" for more information.
>>> ============================ RESTART ============================
>>>
[[1 0 0]
 [0 0 3]
 [0 0 0]]

  (0, 0)        1
  (1, 2)        3
[[1 0 0]
 [0 0 3]
 [0 0 0]]

>>>
```

Ln: 17 Col: 4

FIGURE 3.76   Output of Python Program to Demonstrate a Sparse Matrix.

The following example demonstrates how to compute sparsity and density for a given matrix. This is illustrated in Figure 3.77 and Figure 3.78.

```
File Edit Format Run Options Windows Help
import numpy as np
from scipy.sparse import csr_matrix
a=np.array([[1,0,0],[0,0,3],[0,0,0]])
print(a,"\n")
nonzero_ele = np.count_nonzero(a)
total_ele=np.product(a.shape)
density=(nonzero_ele/total_ele)*100
sparsity=((total_ele - nonzero_ele)/total_ele)*100
print("Sparsity: ",sparsity,"%")
print("Density: ",density,"%")
                                                          Ln: 12 Col: 0
```

FIGURE 3.77 Python Program to Compute Sparsity and Density for a Given Matrix.

```
File Edit Shell Debug Options Windows Help
Python 3.4.2 (default, Sep 26 2018, 07:16:01)
[GCC 4.9.2] on linux
Type "copyright", "credits" or "license()" for more information.
>>> ================================ RESTART ================================
>>>
[[1 0 0]
 [0 0 3]
 [0 0 0]]

Sparsity:  77.7777777778 %
Density:  22.2222222222 %
>>>
                                                          Ln: 12 Col: 4
```

FIGURE 3.78 Output of Python Program to Compute Sparsity and Density for a Given Matrix.

3.22.3 Inverse of a Matrix

The module that supports Linear Algebra in SciPy is linalg. Let us compute the inverse of matrix using SciPy

$$
\begin{matrix}
1 & 2 & 3 \\
0 & 1 & 5 \\
5 & 6 & 0
\end{matrix}
$$

The inverse of the above matrix is

$$
\begin{array}{rrr}
-6 & 3.6 & 1.4 \\
5 & -3 & -1 \\
-1 & 0.8 & 0.2
\end{array}
$$

File Edit Format Run Options Windows Help

```
import numpy as np
from scipy import linalg
square_mat=np.array([[1,2,3],
                     [0,1,5],
                     [5,6,0]])
print("Square Matrix: ")
print(square_mat)
inv_mat=linalg.inv(square_mat)
print("Inverse Matrix: ")
print(inv_mat)
```

Ln: 12 Col: 0

FIGURE 3.79   Python Program to Compute Inverse of Matrix.

File Edit Shell Debug Options Windows Help

```
Python 3.4.2 (default, Sep 26 2018, 07:16:01)
[GCC 4.9.2] on linux
Type "copyright", "credits" or "license()" for more information.
>>> ============================== RESTART ==============================
>>>
Square Matrix:
[[1 2 3]
 [0 1 5]
 [5 6 0]]
Inverse Matrix:
[[-6.    3.6  1.4]
 [ 5.   -3.  -1. ]
 [-1.    0.8  0.2]]
>>>
```

Ln: 14 Col: 4

FIGURE 3.80   Output of Python Program to Compute Inverse of Matrix.

3.22.4 Cholesky Decomposition

The **Cholesky decomposition** or **Cholesky factorization** is a decomposition of a Hermitian, positive-definite matrix into the product of a lower triangular matrix and its conjugate transpose.

```
File Edit Format Run Options Windows Help
import numpy as np
from scipy import linalg
mat=np.array([[4,12,-16],
              [12,37,-43],
              [-16,-43,98]])
print("Input Matrix: ")
print(mat)
inv_mat=linalg.cholesky(mat)
print("Output Matrix: ")
print(inv_mat)

                                                            Ln: 12 Col: 0
```

FIGURE 3.81   Python Program to Compute Cholesky Decomposition.

```
File Edit Shell Debug Options Windows Help
Python 3.4.2 (default, Sep 26 2018, 07:16:01)
[GCC 4.9.2] on linux
Type "copyright", "credits" or "license()" for more information.
>>> ============================ RESTART ================================
>>>
Input Matrix:
[[  4  12 -16]
 [ 12  37 -43]
 [-16 -43  98]]
Output Matrix:
[[ 2.   6.  -8.]
 [ 0.   1.   5.]
 [ 0.   0.   3.]]
>>>

                                                            Ln: 14 Col: 4
```

FIGURE 3.82   Output of Python Program to Compute Cholesky Decomposition.

3.22.5 Application to Visualize Student Study Hours Using SciPy

Suppose a student studies a fixed number of hours per day. His hours of study may vary. The data is given by a csv file, as illustrated in Figure 3.83.

```
File Edit Search Options Help
1,3
2,3.5
3,4
4,4.5
5,5
8,5.5
9,4.5
10,4
11,3.5
12,4
```

FIGURE 3.83   Snapshot of student.csv File.

SciPy genfromtxt can be used to read data from a text file; in this case, it is a CSV file. Python's slice operator is used to split columns into x and y. Then we use Matplotlib functions to plot the study pattern. This is illustrated in Figure 3.84.

```
File  Edit  Format  Run  Options  Windows  Help
import scipy as sp
import matplotlib.pyplot as plt
info=sp.genfromtxt("student.csv", delimiter=",")
x = info[:,0]
y = info[:,1]
x_axis = x
y_axis = y
plt.rcParams['toolbar'] = 'None'
fig = plt.figure()
axes = fig.add_axes([0.1, 0.1, 1, 1])
axes.set_xlim(0, 14)
axes.set_ylim(0, 8)
axes.plot(x_axis, y_axis)
plt.xlabel("Days")
plt.ylabel("Hours")
plt.show()

                                                          Ln: 18 Col: 0
```

FIGURE 3.84   Python Matplotlib Code to Plot Student Study Pattern.

The output plot is as follows and is illustrated in Figure 3.85.

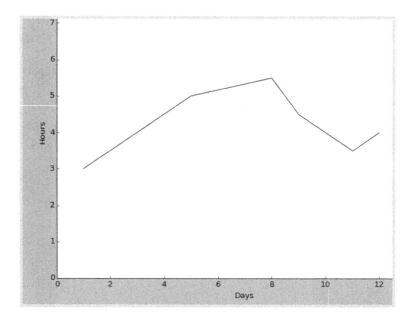

FIGURE 3.85   Output of Python Matplotlib Code to Plot Student Study Pattern.

The line graph shows the student's study pattern in terms of hours for 12 days.

3.23 MATPLOTLIB INTRODUCTION

Matplotlib is a 2-D plotting package available for Python programmers. For data analysts and machine-intelligence algorithm designers, plotting data characterization and outputs in terms of graphs is essential. These things are taken care of by Matplotlib, which is a huge library.

```
File  Edit  Shell  Debug  Options  Windows  Help
Python 3.4.2 (default, Sep 26 2018, 07:16:01)
[GCC 4.9.2] on linux
Type "copyright", "credits" or "license()" for more information.
>>> import matplotlib.pyplot as plt
>>>
                                                            Ln: 5 Col: 4
```

FIGURE 3.86   Python Command Code to Test Whether Matplotlib Is Properly Installed.

If importing Matplotlib and its module pyplot as a plt returns the command interpreter prompt, that means that Matplotlib has been installed properly.

3.23.1 Exploring Matplotlib

The basic types of plots in Matplotlib are line plots, scatterplots and histograms. Let us first consider line plots.

Line plots plot lines co-relating x with corresponding y values. The example in Figure 3.87 illustrates a line plot.

```
File  Edit  Format  Run  Options  Windows  Help
import matplotlib.pyplot as plt
import numpy as np
x=[1,2,3,4,5]
y=[9,8,3,6,7]
plt.rcParams['toolbar'] = 'None'
plt.plot(x,y)
plt.show()
                                                            Ln: 9 Col: 0
```

FIGURE 3.87   Python Matplotlib Code to Plot a Line Plot.

The method plot() takes x and y coordinates for plotting. The show() method is used to display the plot in a new window. As we do not want the toolbars to be displayed, we are making use of a statement **plt. rcParams['toolbarv']** = **'None'**. To change the default rc settings of a Matplotlib, we have a dictionary type variable matplotlib.rcParams, in which all of the default settings are available. Thus in our case we have disabled the toolbar by setting it to none.

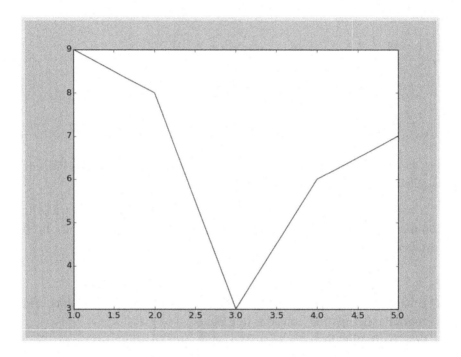

FIGURE 3.88   Output of Python Matplotlib Code to Plot a Line Plot.

Our next step would be to give a name to the x-axis and y-axis, give a title to the graph, set the limits to the x-axis and y-axis and change the line color.

```
File Edit Format Run Options Windows Help
import matplotlib.pyplot as plt
import numpy as np
x=[1,2,3,4,5]
y=[9,8,3,6,7]
plt.rcParams['toolbar'] = 'None'
plt.title('Simple line graph')
plt.xlabel('X axis')
plt.ylabel('Y axis')
plt.plot(x,y,"red")
plt.xlim(0,6)
plt.ylim(0, 10)
plt.show()


                                                    Ln: 14 Col: 0
```

FIGURE 3.89   Python Matplotlib Code to Plot a Named Line Plot with Axis Labels.

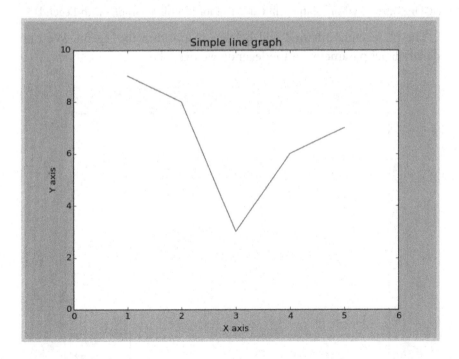

FIGURE 3.90   Output of Python Matplotlib Code to Plot a Named Line Plot with Axis Labels.

Next, we plot multiline graphs with legends giving information about the plots.

```
File  Edit  Format  Run  Options  Windows  Help
import matplotlib.pyplot as plt
import numpy as np
x=[1,2,3,4,5]
y=[9,8,3,6,7]
x1=[1,3,5,7,8]
y1=[7,6,3,8,9]
plt.rcParams['toolbar'] = 'None'
plt.title('Multi-line graph')
plt.xlabel('X axis')
plt.ylabel('Y axis')
p=plt.plot(x,y,"red",label="line1")
q=plt.plot(x1,y1,"green",label="line2")
plt.xlim(0,10)
plt.ylim(0, 10)
plt.legend(loc='lower right')
plt.show()
```

Ln: 18 Col: 0

FIGURE 3.91   Python Matplotlib Code to Plot Multiline Graphs with Legends.

The plt.legend() method will help us to position the legend. We can specify label parameter to the legends we describe.

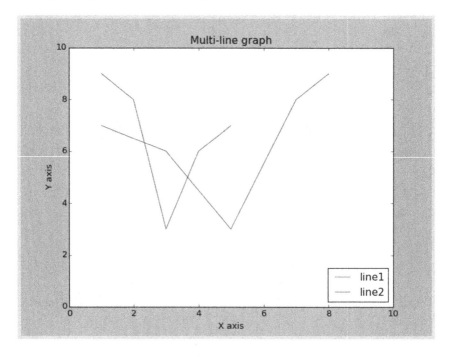

FIGURE 3.92   Output of Python Matplotlib Code to Plot Multiline Graphs with Legends.

Now we apply Matplotlib to draw a scatter plot. This is illustrated in Figure 3.93.

```
File  Edit  Format  Run  Options  Windows  Help
import matplotlib.pyplot as plt
import numpy as np
x=[1,2,3,4,5]
y=[9,8,3,6,7]
plt.rcParams['toolbar'] = 'None'
plt.scatter(x,y,c="red")
plt.title('Scatter Plot')
plt.xlabel('X axis')
plt.ylabel('Y axis')
plt.show()




                                                            Ln: 12 Col: 0
```

FIGURE 3.93   Python Matplotlib Code to Plot Scatter Plot.

Here we use the plt.scatter() method, and we use the parameter c to assign the color.

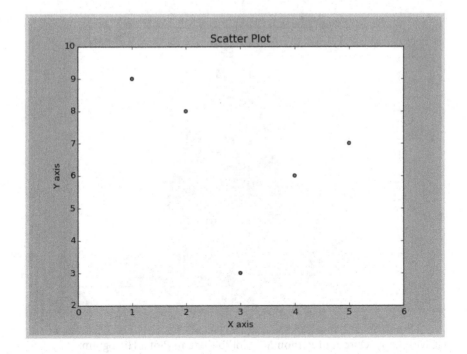

FIGURE 3.94   Output of Python Matplotlib Code to Plot Scatter Plot.

Now we try to plot a histogram using Matplotlib. This is illustrated in Figure 3.95.

```
File  Edit  Format  Run  Options  Windows  Help
import matplotlib.pyplot as plt
import numpy as np
y = np.random.randn(100)*0.05
plt.rcParams['toolbar'] = 'None'
plt.hist(y,14, alpha=0.5, histtype='bar', ec='black');
plt.show()


                                                    Ln: 8 Col: 0
```

FIGURE 3.95 Python Matplotlib Code to Plot a Histogram.

Here we use plt.hist() method. The opacity is set with the alpha parameter, histtype is bar and the edge color is set to black. The output is illustrated in Figure 3.96.

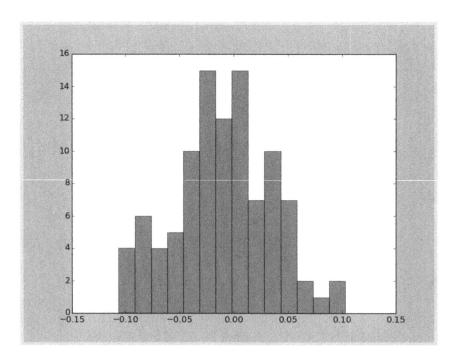

FIGURE 3.96 Output of Python Matplotlib Code to Plot a Histogram.

EXERCISE

Answer the following briefly

1. Is Python a compiled or interpreted programming language?

2. Is there any char datatype in Python?

3. What is the role of + operator in Python?

4. Explain the role of else with respect to while and for loop.

5. Which sorting algorithm does Python's sort() function follow?

6. Are tuples in Python mutable?

7. Can Python list store heterogeneous data?

8. Can a Python dictionary have multiple keys for a given value?

9. How do you create an array using NumPy?

10. Is a Pandas series 1-dimensional or 2-dimensional array?

11. Can a Pandas DataFrame's rows and columns be labeled?

12. What does CSV stand for on a file?

13. How do you get the number of rows and columns in a CSV file?

14. What useful functions does the SciPy library provide?

15. For what purpose are density plots used?

16. What is a scatter plot used for?

17. Which Python library you would use to plot graphs?

SOLVE THE FOLLOWING

1. Write a Python program that accepts a multiline sentence and gives the frequency of occurrence of the top 10 words. Stop words should not be counted.

2. Write a Python program to initialize a NumPy array with values 10, 20, 30, 40 and 50 and compute the mean.

3. Write a Python program to demonstrate the time consumed by operations on a Python List versus similar operations performed on a NumPy array.

4. Write a Python program using the Pandas library to read the state. csv as given in Figure 3.97 and generate its summary statistics.

```
File  Edit  Format  Run  Options  Windows  Help
Montgomery,9.20,198232,Alabhama
Tallahassee,6.66,193078,Florida
Baton Rouge,8.70,226505,Louisiana
Boston,6.69,687584,Massachusetts
Richmond,7.15,230254,Virginia

                                                    Ln: 6 Col: 0
```

FIGURE 3.97   Snapshot of state.csv file.

5. Write a Python program using the SciPy library to compute the determinant of an array

$$1 \quad 2 \quad 3$$
$$4 \quad 5 \quad 6$$
$$7 \quad 8 \quad 9$$

6. Write a Python program using Matplotlib and considering a suitable example to plot a 3-dimensional line graph.

## CHAPTER 4

Machine Learning

4.0 WHAT IS MEANT BY MACHINE LEARNING?

In machine learning, algorithms attempt to learn without explicit instructions and human interventions and only through experiences.

4.1 CATEGORIES OF MACHINE LEARNING

Machine learning algorithms are classified as

- Supervised

- Unsupervised

- Reinforcement Learning

4.1.1 Supervised Learning

Supervised algorithms learn from labeled data. In supervised learning, there are sets of defined inputs and outputs; through multiple iterations, supervised learning algorithms come up with a function that helps to correctly conclude an output for a given set of inputs that were not part of training data.

4.1.2 Unsupervised Learning

Unsupervised algorithms work with unlabeled data. Here the algorithms are provided only with data, and they try to find the interesting patterns in this data. Unsupervised learning tries to find the commonalities in the data; for a new sample, it tries to find the presence or absence of the discovered commonalities.

4.1.3 Reinforcement Learning

In reinforcement learning, we have agents that interact with an environment to maximize its rewards. It is like learning with a critic. For correct decisions, the agent is rewarded; for wrong decisions, the agent is penalized. Thus, the goal for an agent would be to maximize rewards and reach the goal state.

The machine learning algorithms of supervised, unsupervised and reinforcement learning are illustrated in Figure 4.1

In this book, we discuss the classification of Supervised Machine Learning algorithms.

4.2 CLASSIFICATION IN MACHINE LEARNING

In classification, we try to predict categorical values. The labels for these categorical values come up with a finite set of classes.

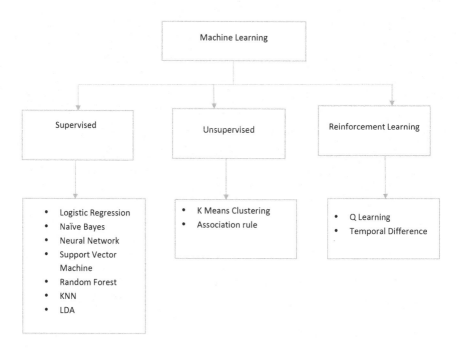

FIGURE 4.1 Categories of Machine Learning Algorithms.

Examples:

- Given an image, predict cat or dog.

- Given an email, predict spam or real.

In binary classification, we have only two classes for prediction, usually with values 0 and 1.

In multi classification, we have more than two classes for prediction (e.g., cat, dog or deer).

In this chapter, we apply the following algorithms for classification problems

1. Logistic Regression

2. Naïve Bayes

3. Neural Network

4. Support Vector Machine

5. Random Forest

6. K N N

7. Linear Discriminate Analysis (LDA)

4.2.1 Metrics for Classification

The following metrics have been used to evaluate the supervised algorithms as mentioned section 4.2.

4.2.1.1 K-Fold Cross-Validation

Cross-validation is an important technique used to validate the performance of a given model. Cross-validation involves keeping a sample of the dataset for testing and training the model on the remaining part of the dataset.

The value k determines the number of groups into which data can be split. We have set the value of k to 10. Thus, it is called 10-fold cross-validation.

A value of k equaling 10 is the most popular value for validating the accuracy of models.

4.2.1.2 Confusion Matrix

A confusion matrix (sometimes known as an error matrix) allows us to analyze the performance of a machine-learning algorithm in a matrix format. Rows represent the predicted class, while columns represent the actual class.

The confusion matrix layout is as depicted in Figure 4.2

TP stands for True Positive: the prediction is yes, and it is true.

TN stands for True Negative: the prediction is no, and it is false.

FN stands for False Negative: the prediction is no, and it is true.

FP stands for False Positive: the prediction is yes, and it is false.

Accuracy determines the correctness of the confusion matrix; it is given in Equation 4.1

$$accuracy = \frac{(TP + TN)}{total}, \tag{4.1}$$

where the total is the row sum of the Predicted or the column sum of the Actuals.

Precision gives the correctness of Prediction when it is Yes and is given in Equation 4.2

$$precision = \frac{(TP)}{Predicted\ Yes}, \tag{4.2}$$

where Predicted Yes is the row sum of Predicted Yes values.

Recall is the capacity of the model to find data points of interest and is given in Equation 4.3

		Actual Values	
Predicted Values		Positive (Yes)	Negative (No)
	Positive (Yes)	TP	FP
	Negative (No)	FN	TN

FIGURE 4.2 Confusion Matrix Layout.

$$recall = \frac{TP}{(TP + FN)}. \qquad (4.3)$$

4.3 REGRESSION

In regression, we try to predict continuous valued output. Machine learning algorithms that predict continuous valued outputs are

- Linear Regression

- Multiple Linear Regression

- Support Vector Machine (applied for both regression and classification)

4.4 SCIKIT-LEARN

Scikit-learn is a library for Python Programming language that supports machine learning. It supports machine-learning features like classification, regression and clustering along with APIs to support popular algorithms like

1. Linear Regression

2. Logistic Regression

3. Naive Bayes

4. Neural Network

5. Support Vector Machine

6. Random Forest

7. K N N

8. LDA

4.4.1 Dataset

We have analyzed the heart disease data set from University of California, Irvine. For our classification tests, we used only 14 attributes, listed in Table 4.1.

The snapshot of the heart disease csv file is illustrated in Figure 4.3

TABLE 4.1 Description of heart disease dataset attributes

Sl_No	Attribute Name	Attribute Name and Description
1	age	Age in years
2	sex	Sex (1 = male; 0 = female)
3	cp	Chest pain type
		• Value 1: typical angina
		• Value 2: atypical angina
		• Value 3: non-anginal pain
		• Value 4: asymptomatic
4	trestbps	resting blood pressure (in mm Hg on admission to the hospital)
5	chol	serum cholesterol in mg/dl
6	fbs	(fasting blood sugar > 120 mg/dl) (1 = true; 0 = false)
7	restecg	resting electrocardiographic results
		• Value 0: normal
		• Value 1: having ST-T wave abnormality (T wave inversions and/or ST elevation or depression of > 0.05 mV)
		• Value 2: showing probable or definite left ventricular hypertrophy by Estes' criteria
8	thalach	maximum heart rate achieved
9	exang	exercise induced angina (1 = yes; 0 = no)
10	oldpeak	ST depression induced by exercise relative to rest
11	slope	the slope of the peak exercise ST segment
		• Value 1: upsloping
		• Value 2: flat
		• Value 3: downsloping
12	ca	number of major vessels (0–3) colored by fluoroscopy
13	thal	3 = normal; 6 = fixed defect; 7 = reversible defect
14	num	diagnosis of heart disease (angiographic disease status)
		• Value 0: < 50% diameter narrowing
		• Value 1: > 50% diameter narrowing
		• (in any major vessel: attributes 59 through 68 are vessels)

```
File Edit Search Options Help
63,1,3,145,233,1,0,150,0,2.3,0,0,1,1
37,1,2,130,250,0,1,187,0,3.5,0,0,2,1
41,0,1,130,204,0,0,172,0,1.4,2,0,2,1
56,1,1,120,236,0,1,178,0,0.8,2,0,2,1
57,0,0,120,354,0,1,163,1,0.6,2,0,2,1
57,1,0,140,192,0,1,148,0,0.4,1,0,1,1
56,0,1,140,294,0,0,153,0,1.3,1,0,2,1
44,1,1,120,263,0,1,173,0,0,2,0,3,1
52,1,2,172,199,1,1,162,0,0.5,2,0,3,1
57,1,2,150,168,0,1,174,0,1.6,2,0,2,1
54,1,0,140,239,0,1,160,0,1.2,2,0,2,1
48,0,2,130,275,0,1,139,0,0.2,2,0,2,1
49,1,1,130,266,0,1,171,0,0.6,2,0,2,1
64,1,3,110,211,0,0,144,1,1.8,1,0,2,1
58,0,3,150,283,1,0,162,0,1,2,0,2,1
50,0,2,120,219,0,1,158,0,1.6,1,0,2,1
58,0,2,120,340,0,1,172,0,0,2,0,2,1
66,0,3,150,226,0,1,114,0,2.6,0,0,2,1
43,1,0,150,247,0,1,171,0,1.5,2,0,2,1
69,0,3,140,239,0,1,151,0,1.8,2,2,2,1
59,1,0,135,234,0,1,161,0,0.5,1,0,3,1
44,1,2,130,233,0,1,179,1,0.4,2,0,2,1
42,1,0,140,226,0,1,178,0,0,2,0,2,1
```

FIGURE 4.3 Snapshot heart.csv file.

4.4.1.1 Analysis of the Dataset

Check how many rows and columns are in the dataset.

Python program: Datashape.py

```
File Edit Format Run Options Windows Help
from pandas import read_csv
filename = "heart.csv"
names = ['age','sex','cp','trestbps','chol','fbs','restecg','thalach','exang','o
        'slope','ca','thal','target']
data = read_csv(filename, names=names)
shape = data.shape
print(shape)
                                                              Ln: 9 Col: 0
```

FIGURE 4.4 Python Program Datashape.py to Analyze heart.csv.

Output

```
File Edit Shell Debug Options Windows Help
Python 3.4.2 (default, Sep 26 2018, 07:16:01)
[GCC 4.9.2] on linux
Type "copyright", "credits" or "license()" for more information.
>>> ============================== RESTART ==============================
>>>
(303, 14)
>>>
                                                              Ln: 7 Col: 4
```

FIGURE 4.5 Output of Python Program Datashape.py.

We observe from the output that the heart disease dataset considered for classification has 303 rows and 14 columns. It is very important to know the attributes of all data, as illustrated in the Python program seen in Figure 4.6 and its output illustrated in Figure 4.7.

Python program: Datatype.py

```
File Edit Format Run Options Windows Help
from pandas import read_csv
filename = "heart.csv"
names = ['age','sex','cp','trestbps','chol','fbs','restecg','thalach','exang','o
        'slope','ca','thal','target']
dat = read_csv(filename, names=names)
attrib_types = dat.dtypes
print(attrib_types)

                                                                    Ln: 9 Col: 0
```

FIGURE 4.6   Python Program to Print the Datatype of Each Attribute.

Output

```
File Edit Shell Debug Options Windows Help
Python 3.4.2 (default, Sep 26 2018, 07:16:01)
[GCC 4.9.2] on linux
Type "copyright", "credits" or "license()" for more information.
>>> ================================ RESTART ================================
>>>
age            int64
sex            int64
cp             int64
trestbps       int64
chol           int64
fbs            int64
restecg        int64
thalach        int64
exang          int64
oldpeak        float64
slope          int64
ca             int64
thal           int64
target         int64
dtype: object
>>>

                                                                    Ln: 21 Col: 4
```

FIGURE 4.7   Output of Python Program to Print the Datatype of Each Attribute.

4.4.1.2 Correlation

Correlation indicates the relatedness among variables. It generally speaks about what one variable knows about the other. The performance of machine learning, like linear and logistic regression, will be affected if they have highly correlated data.

4.4.1.3 Pearson Correlation

Pearson correlation is a measure of the linear relationship between two variables (A and B). A value of 1 indicates positive correlation, -1 indicates negative correlation and 0 indicates no linear correlation. The Pearson correlation is as given in Equation 4.4

$$P_{A,B} = \frac{Cov(A, B)}{\sigma A \; \sigma B},\qquad(4.4)$$

where Cov is the covariance,
σA is the standard deviation of A and
σB is the standard deviation of B.

Python program: Pcovdata.py

```
File Edit Format Run Options Windows Help
import matplotlib.pyplot as plt
from pandas import read_csv
import numpy
filename = "heart.csv"
names = ['age','sex','cp','trestbps','chol','fbs','restecg','thalach','exang',
         'oldpeak','slope','ca','thal','target']
dat = read_csv(filename, names=names)
correlations = dat.corr(method='pearson')
plt.rcParams['toolbar'] = 'None'
fig = plt.figure()
ax = fig.add_subplot(111)
cax = ax.matshow(correlations, vmin=-1, vmax=1)
fig.colorbar(cax)
ticks = numpy.arange(0,13,1)
ax.set_xticks(ticks)
ax.set_yticks(ticks)
ax.set_xticklabels(names)
ax.set_yticklabels(names)
plt.xticks(rotation=70)#to see that labels dont overlap
plt.show()
                                                      Ln: 22 Col: 0
```

FIGURE 4.8   Python Program Pcovdata.py to Generate Covariance Matrix.

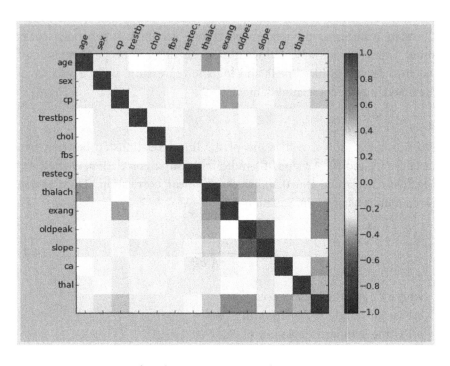

FIGURE 4.9 Output of Python Program Pcovdata.py to Generate Covariance Matrix.

The matrix displays positive covariance, as you can see in the diagonal line from left top to right bottom.

4.4.2 Check whether Scikit-learn is properly installed

Run the statement on the idle editor in Python as illustrated in Figure 4.10.

```
File Edit Shell Debug Options Windows Help
Python 3.4.2 (default, Sep 26 2018, 07:16:01)
[GCC 4.9.2] on linux
Type "copyright", "credits" or "license()" for more information.
>>> import sklearn
>>>
                                                          Ln: 5 Col: 4
```

FIGURE 4.10 Python Program to Check Whether Scikit-learn Is Properly Installed.

If we get the interpreter prompt without any error that means Scikit-learn has been installed properly.

4.4.3 Procedure for Loading the Data

The given dataset is available as csv file.

```
from pandas import read_csv
filename = 'heart.csv'
names = ['age', 'sex', 'cp', 'trestbps', 'chol', 'fbs', 'restecg', 'thalach', 'exang', 'oldpeak',
    'ca', 'thal', 'target']
data = read_csv(filename, names=names)
```

The **read_csv()** function helps you to load a CSV file into a Pandas DataFrame.

4.4.4 Splitting Data into Training and Testing

This is the procedure:

```
from sklearn.model_selection import train_test_split
X = array[:,0:13]
Y = array[:,13]
X_train, X_test, y_train, y_test = train_test_split(X, Y, test_size = 0.2,
    random_state = 0)
```

The train_test_split()function is used to split the data into training and testing subsets. The percentage of split in the function is 80/20 (i.e., 80% for training and 20% for testing).

The random_state is set to an integer that will act as a seed for the random number generator during the split.

4.4.5 Building the Models for Supervised Learning

- **Logistic Regression**

  ```
  from sklearn.linear_model import LogisticRegression
  reg = LogisticRegression()
  ```

  Here reg is an object of the class LogisticRegression()

- **Naive Bayes**

  ```
  from sklearn.naive_bayes import GaussianNB
  nbmodel = GaussianNB()
  ```

  Here nbmodel is an object of the class LogisticRegression()

- **Neural Network MLP**
  from sklearn.neural_network import MLPClassifier
  mlp = MLPClassifier(hidden_layer_sizes=(30, 30, 30), max_iter=1000)

  where *hidden_layer_sizes=(30, 30, 30)* defines the layers of the Neural Network
  max_iter=1000 defines the iterations for training over the dataset.

- **Support Vector Machine (SVM)**
  from sklearn.svm import SVC
  svmodel=SVC(kernel='linear',probability=True)

  where *kernel='linear' means* it will be a Linear SVC model and is useful in a dataset that has a high number of features.
  *probability=*True. If you want to generate predicted probabilities, Probability must be set to True.

- **Random Forest**
  from sklearn.ensemble import RandomForestClassifier
  clf = RandomForestClassifier()

  where clf means a classifier is an object of the class RandomForestClassifier.

- **K Neighbors**
  from sklearn.neighbors import KNeighborsClassifier
  knclf = KNeighborsClassifier(n_neighbors=5)

  where n_neighbors are the number of neighbors set to 5.

- **Linear Discriminant Analysis (LDA)**
  from sklearn.discriminant_analysis import LinearDiscriminantAnalysis
  ldac = LinearDiscriminantAnalysis()

  where ldac means a classifier is an object of the class LDA.

4.4.6 Model Fitting, Scaling and Prediction in Supervised Learning

Model fitting is equivalent to training the model with the training data. Let us see how various models are trained. For a classification, you can classify the test data with the predict method

- **Logistic Regression**
  reg.fit(X_train, y_train)
  y_pred = reg.predict(X_test)

  Here, the *reg.fit(X_train, y_train)* is used to train the classifier model; prediction for new data instances is done with the *reg. predict(X_test)* method.

- **Naive Bayes**
  The training and prediction are similar to that in logistic regression.

  r=nbmodel.fit(X_train, y_train)
  y_pred = nbmodel.predict(X_test)

- **Neural Network MLP**
  If your data has different scales, it is helpful to normalize and rescale the data. Feature scaling is done only on the training data; the test data is kept as close to reality as possible as seen in *scaler.fit (X_train)*.

  from sklearn.neural_network import MLPClassifier
  scaler = StandardScaler()
  scaler.fit(X_train)
  X_train = scaler.transform(X_train)
  X_test = scaler.transform(X_test)
  r=mlp.fit(X_train, y_train)
  y_pred = mlp.predict(X_test)

  The transform function is used to compute the mean and standard deviation on the training set so that you can apply it to the testing set.

- **Support Vector Machine (SVM)**
  The training of the SVM classifier is done with the fit() function for the training data; the prediction of the trained classifier is done with the predict() function for the testing data.

  r=svmodel.fit(X_train, y_train)
  y_pred = svmodel.predict(X_test)

- **Random Forest**
  from sklearn.ensemble import RandomForestClassifier
  stdc = StandardScaler()
  X_train = stdc.fit_transform(X_train)
  X_test = stdc.transform(X_test)
  r=clf.fit(X_train, y_train)
  y_pred = clf.predict(X_test)

The Standard Scaler is applied for the Random Forest feature scaling of training data and is further transformed. Once it is done, the model classifier is trained on the training data and tested for predictions on the predict() function.

- **K Neighbors**
  from sklearn.preprocessing import StandardScaler
  ksc = StandardScaler()
  ksc.fit(X_train)
  X_train = ksc.transform(X_train)
  X_test = ksc.transform(X_test)
  r=knclf.fit(X_train, y_train)
  y_pred = knclf.predict(X_test)

The Standard Scaler is applied for the K Nearest Neighbor feature scaling of training data and is further transformed. Once it is done, the model classifier is trained on the training data and tested for predictions on the predict() function.

- **Linear Discriminant Analysis (LDA)**
  from sklearn.preprocessing import StandardScaler
  lsc = StandardScaler()
  lsc.fit(X_train)
  X_train = lsc.transform(X_train)
  X_test = lsc.transform(X_test)
  r = ldac.fit_transform(X_train, y_train)
  y_pred = ldac.predict(X_test)

The Standard Scaler is applied for LDA and the feature scaling of its training data that is further transformed. Once it is done, the model classifier is trained on the training data and tested for predictions on the predict() function.

4.4.7 K-Fold Classification Accuracy with Scikit-learn.

```
from sklearn.model_selection import KFold
num_folds = 10
kfold = KFold(n_splits=10, random_state=7)
results = cross_val_score(reg, X, Y, cv=kfold)
print("K-Fold Classification Accuracy:",results.mean()*100,"%")
```

In our experimentation, we have used 10-fold K Cross Validation. Here 1 fold is used for validation whereas 10–1 = 9 folds are used for training; this is repeated for all combinations. Compute the cross validation scores with the function *cross_val_score()*.Finally, compute the accuracy as the mean of results.

4.4.8 Confusion Matrix Implementation with Sckit-learn.

A confusion matrix provides insights into the classification algorithm. The Scikit code is

```
from sklearn import metrics
conf_matrix = metrics.confusion_matrix(y_test, y_pred)
print(conf_matrix)
print("Confusion Matrix Accuracy:",metrics.accuracy_score(y_test, y_pred)*
    100,"%")
print("Confusion Matrix Precision:",metrics.precision_score(y_test, y_pred)*
    100,"%")
print("Confusion Matrix Recall:",metrics.recall_score(y_test, y_pred)*100,"%")
```

Consider the following confusion matrix generated Logistic Regression example

[[22 5]

[4 30]]

The diagonal elements show the classifications for each class. Thus, for class 0 we have 22 correct predictions and for class 1 we have 30 accurate predictions.

The off diagonal shows the wrong classifications.

Thus, accuracy is correctly classified/all classified = (52/61)* 100 = 85.2459.

4.4.9 ROC Curve

The ROC curve is used to balance between True Positives and False positives. The code to plot ROC is

```
y_pred_prob = reg.predict_proba(X_test)[::,1]
fp_rate, tp_rate, _ = metrics.roc_curve(y_test, y_pred_prob)
auc_score = metrics.roc_auc_score(y_test, y_pred_prob)
plt.rcParams['toolbar'] = 'None'
plt.title('Logistic Regression')
plt.xlabel('False Positive Rate')
plt.ylabel('True Positive Rate')
plt.plot(fp_rate,tp_rate,label="data 1, auc="+str(auc_score))
plt.legend(loc=4)
plt.show()
```

The prediction of probabilities is done with the reg.predict_proba() function. We restrict it to only positive outcomes. We compute the Area Under Curve(AUC) and Receiver Operating Characteristic curve (RUC) with the functions *metrics.roc_auc_score(y_test, y_pred_prob)* *metrics.roc_curve(y_test, y_pred_prob)* and plot the same.

If AUC is 0, the outcome is bad; if AUC is 1, the outcome is good.

4.5 LOGISTIC REGRESSION

Logistic regression is also a supervised learning technique. It is more suitable as a classification technique rather than as a regression technique. Logistic regression is more often applied to discrete classes. Examples of discrete classes are male/female, cat/dog and pass/fail. Logistic regression models its output as a logistic sigmoid function, which maps to the discrete classes.

The mathematical modeling of logistic regression is as follows in Equation 4.5.

$$y_d = \log\left(P/_{1-p}\right)$$
$$= \gamma_0 + \gamma_1 * x_1 + \gamma_2 * x_2 + - - - - - - - \gamma_n * x_m, \tag{4.5}$$

where p is the probability that $y_d = 1$ given the values of the vector of the input features x

$\gamma_0, \gamma_1, \gamma_2 -------- \gamma_n$ are estimated through the maximum likelihood function.

$x_1, x_2, -------- x_m$ are vectors of the input features.

γ_n is known as the vector of coefficients.

4.5.1 Logistic Regression Sigmoid Function

The sigmoid function used in logistic regression is shown in Figure 4.11.

The sigmoid function maps any real value to a value between 0 and 1. The sigmoid function is given by the Equation 4.6.

$$S(y) = \frac{1}{1 + e^{-y}}, \tag{4.6}$$

where $S(y)$ is a value between 0 and 1.

y is the input to the function.

e is the base to the natural log.

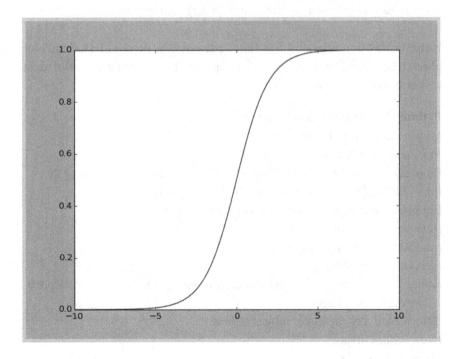

FIGURE 4.11   Sigmoid Curve.

4.5.2 Types of Logistic Regression

- **Binary logistic regression:** This type of logistic regression models two outcomes only (e.g., pass and fail).

- **Multinomial logistic regression:** This type of logistic regression models three or more outcomes without any ordering (e.g., cats, dogs and sheep).

- **Ordinal logistic regression:** This type of logistic regression models three or more outcomes with ordering (e.g., product ratings from 1 to 5).

To apply logistic regression, the dataset should ideally support the following properties

- The independent variables need to be independent of each other.

- Proper and meaningful variables need to be considered for modeling logistic regression.

- Logistic regression usually requires large sample sizes.

Note: If logistic regression has fewer parameters, there is less chance of overfitting. Overfitting analysis corresponds to a particular set of data and may fail for additional data.

Python Program: Logisticregrr.py

```
from pandas import read_csv
from sklearn.model_selection import KFold
from sklearn.model_selection import cross_val_score
from sklearn.linear_model import LogisticRegression
from sklearn.model_selection import train_test_split
from sklearn import metrics
from matplotlib import pyplot as plt
filename = 'heart.csv'
names = ['age','sex','cp','trestbps','chol','fbs','restecg','thalach','exang','oldpeak',
    'slope','ca','thal','target']
data = read_csv(filename, names=names)
types = data.dtypes
array = data.values
X = array[:,0:13]
Y = array[:,13]
```

```
X_train, X_test, y_train, y_test = train_test_split(X, Y, test_size = 0.2,
    random_state = 0)
num_folds = 10
kfold = KFold(n_splits=10, random_state=7)
reg = LogisticRegression()
results = cross_val_score(reg, X, Y, cv=kfold)
print("K-Fold Classification Accuracy:",results.mean()*100,"%")
reg.fit(X_train, y_train)
y_pred = reg.predict(X_test)
conf_matrix = metrics.confusion_matrix(y_test, y_pred)
print(conf_matrix)
print("Confusion Matrix Accuracy:",metrics.accuracy_score(y_test, y_pred)*
    100,"%")
print("Confusion Matrix Precision:",metrics.precision_score(y_test, y_pred)*
    100,"%")
print("Confusion Matrix Recall:",metrics.recall_score(y_test, y_pred)*100,"%")
y_pred_prob = reg.predict_proba(X_test)[::,1]
fp_rate, tp_rate, _ = metrics.roc_curve(y_test, y_pred_prob)
auc_score = metrics.roc_auc_score(y_test, y_pred_prob)
plt.rcParams['toolbar'] = 'None'
plt.title('Logistic Regression')
plt.xlabel('False Positive Rate')
plt.ylabel('True Positive Rate')
plt.plot(fp_rate,tp_rate,label="data 1, auc="+str(auc_score))
plt.legend(loc=4)
plt.show()
```

Output

```
File Edit Shell Debug Options Windows Help
Python 3.4.2 (default, Sep 26 2018, 07:16:01)
[GCC 4.9.2] on linux
Type "copyright", "credits" or "license()" for more information.
>>> ============================ RESTART ============================
>>>
K-Fold Classification Accuracy: 79.4516129032 %
[[22  5]
 [ 4 30]]
Confusion Matrix Accuracy: 85.2459016393 %
Confusion Matrix Precision: 85.7142857143 %
Confusion Matrix Recall: 88.2352941176 %



                                                              Ln: 6 Col: 0
```

FIGURE 4.12   Output of Python Program Logisticregrr.py.

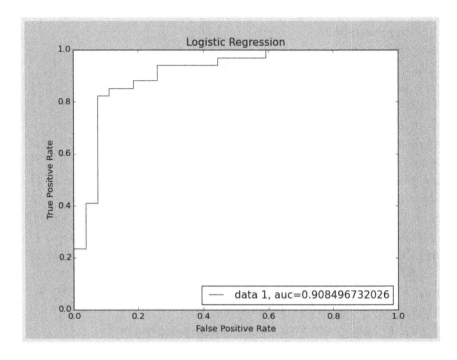

FIGURE 4.13   ROC Curve of Logistic Regression.

4.6 NAIVE BAYES

Naive Bayes is a supervised learning technique. It is a probabilistic classifier based on the Bayes theorem. It represents a classification technique that relies on the independence of the predictors (independent variables).

The term Naive implies that the occurrence of certain feature is independent of other features. The term Bayes tells that the basis of Naive Bayes is the Bayes theorem. Bayes Theorem gives the conditional probability of event X given event Y has occurred, as specified in Equation 4.7.

$$P(X|Y) = \frac{P(Y|X).P(X)}{P(Y)}, \qquad (4.7)$$

where
   $P(X|Y)$ is the conditional probability of X given Y.
   $P(Y|X)$ is the conditional probability of Y given X.

P(X) is the Probability of event X.

P(Y) is the Probability of event Y.

The best feature of Naive Bayes is that it can handle an arbitrary number of independent variables regardless of whether they are independent or continuous.

From a set of variables $X = \{x1, x2, ------- xn\}$ we want to get the posterior probability for the event Cj among the set of outcomes $C = \{c1, c2, -------cn\}$. Here in more generic terms X is the set of predictors, and C is the categorical levels present in the dependent variables.

The final posterior probability is as given Equation 4.8.

$$p(C_j \mid X) \propto p\,(C_j)\prod_{k}^{n} p(x_n \mid C_j). \tag{4.8}$$

4.6.1 Advantages of Naive Bayes

- It builds the model quickly and makes quick decisions.

- It can handle both continuous and discrete data.

- It is highly scalable with respect to the number of predictors and data points.

- Medical Diagnosis

- Weather Prediction

- News Classification

4.6.2 Naive Bayes Applications

- Medical Diagnosis

- Weather Prediction

- News Classification

Python Program: NaiveBayes.py

```
from pandas import read_csv
from sklearn.model_selection import KFold
from sklearn.model_selection import cross_val_score
from sklearn.naive_bayes import GaussianNB
```

```
from sklearn.model_selection import train_test_split
from sklearn import metrics
from matplotlib import pyplot as plt
filename = 'heart.csv'
names = ['age','sex','cp','trestbps','chol','fbs','restecg','thalach','exang','old-
    peak','slope','ca','thal','target']
dataframe = read_csv(filename, names=names)
array = dataframe.values
X = array[:,0:13]
Y = array[:,13]
X_train, X_test, y_train, y_test = train_test_split(X, Y, test_size = 0.2,
    random_state = 0)
kfold = KFold(n_splits=10, random_state=7)
nbmodel = GaussianNB()
results = cross_val_score(nbmodel, X, Y, cv=kfold)
print("K-Fold Classification Accuracy:",results.mean()*100)
r=nbmodel.fit(X_train, y_train)
y_pred = nbmodel.predict(X_test)
conf_matrix = metrics.confusion_matrix(y_test, y_pred)
print(conf_matrix)
print("Confusion Matrix Accuracy:",metrics.accuracy_score(y_test, y_pred)*
    100,"%")
print("Confusion Matrix Precision:",metrics.precision_score(y_test, y_pred)*
    100,"%")
print("Confusion Matrix Recall:",metrics.recall_score(y_test, y_pred)*100,"%")
y_pred_prob = r.predict_proba(X_test)[:,1]
fp_rate, tp_rate, _ = metrics.roc_curve(y_test, y_pred_prob)
auc_score = metrics.roc_auc_score(y_test, y_pred_prob)
plt.rcParams['toolbar'] = 'None'
plt.title('Naive Bayes')
plt.xlabel('False Positive Rate')
plt.ylabel('True Positive Rate')
plt.plot(fp_rate,tp_rate,label="data 1, auc="+str(auc_score))
plt.legend(loc=4)
plt.show()
```

Output

```
File  Edit  Shell  Debug  Options  Windows  Help
Python 3.4.2 (default, Sep 26 2018, 07:16:01)
[GCC 4.9.2] on linux
Type "copyright", "credits" or "license()" for more information.
>>> ================================ RESTART ================================
>>>
K-Fold Classification Accuracy: 80.4731182796
[[21  6]
 [ 3 31]]
Confusion Matrix Accuracy: 85.2459016393 %
Confusion Matrix Precision: 83.7837837838 %
Confusion Matrix Recall: 91.1764705882 %
```
Ln: 6 Col: 0

FIGURE 4.14   Python Program NaiveBayes.py to Implement Naive Bayes.

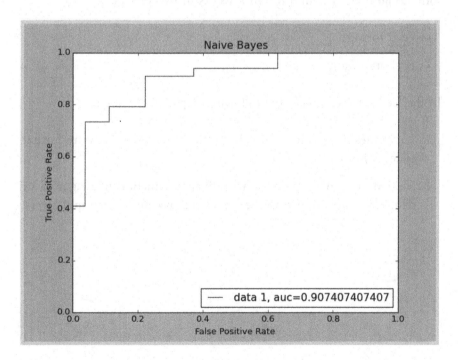

FIGURE 4.15   ROC Curve of Naive Bayes.

4.7 NEURAL NETWORK MLP

Neural network or commonly known as Artificial Neural Network is a system for processing information inspired from biological neural networks. It is made up of numerous processing elements known as neurons that interact with one another to solve a problem.

Neural Networks are classified into 3 categories

- Multi-Layer Perceptron (MLP)
- Convolutional Neural Networks
- Recurrent Neural Network

In our discussion, we consider the MLP classifier, composed of at least three layers of neurons. This is illustrated in Figure 4.16.

LPs are fully connected. Each layer connects to another layer with some weight w_{ij}. A neural network works in two phases.

- Feed forward
- Backpropagation

In the feed forward phase, the following steps are executed.

1. The values in the inputs are multiplied by weights. They are further added with bias.

2. Hidden layer neurons have an activation function like sigmoid or relu. These are applied to the values received from the input layers.

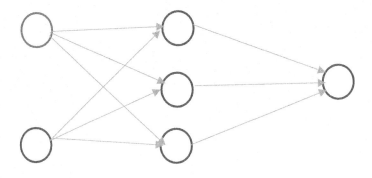

Input Layer   Hidden Layer   Output Layer

FIGURE 4.16 Three Layer Multi-layer Perceptron.

3. The processed values are then given to the output layers. These are the actual outputs of the algorithm.

The outputs generated may need not be accurate. Thus, the backpropagation phase is initiated.

In the backpropagation phase, the following steps are executed.

1. The error is calculated by computing the difference between the output and the input. This difference is known as a loss and the corresponding function as the loss function. An example of the loss function is a mean squared error.

2. A partial derivative of the error function known as the gradient descent is computed. If the slope of the error function is positive, then weights can be reduced or the weights can be increased. This exercise reduces the overall error, and its corresponding function is called the optimization function.

MLPs are suitable for classification problems in which the inputs are assigned a class or label.

4.7.1 Application of MLPs

- Time Series Predictions

- Image Processing

- Character Recognition

Python program: MLP.py

```
from pandas import read_csv
from sklearn.model_selection import KFold
from sklearn.model_selection import cross_val_score
from sklearn.neural_network import MLPClassifier
from sklearn.model_selection import train_test_split
from matplotlib import pyplot as plt
from sklearn import metrics
from sklearn.preprocessing import StandardScaler
filename = 'heart.csv'
```

```
names  =  ['age','sex','cp','trestbps','chol','fbs','restecg','thalach','exang','old-
    peak','slope','ca','thal','target']
dataframe = read_csv(filename, names=names)
array = dataframe.values
X = array[:,0:13]
Y = array[:,13]
X_train, X_test, y_train, y_test = train_test_split(X, Y, test_size = 0.2,
    random_state = 0)
scaler = StandardScaler()
scaler.fit(X_train)
X_train = scaler.transform(X_train)
X_test = scaler.transform(X_test)
mlp = MLPClassifier(hidden_layer_sizes=(30, 30, 30), max_iter=1000)
r=mlp.fit(X_train, y_train)
kfold = KFold(n_splits=10, random_state=7)
results = cross_val_score(mlp, X, Y, cv=kfold)
print("K-Fold Classification Accuracy:",results.mean()*100)
y_pred = mlp.predict(X_test)
conf_matrix = metrics.confusion_matrix(y_test, y_pred)
print(conf_matrix)
print("Confusion Matrix Accuracy:",metrics.accuracy_score(y_test, y_pred)*
    100,"%")
print("Confusion Matrix Precision:",metrics.precision_score(y_test, y_pred)*
    100,"%")
print("Confusion Matrix Recall:",metrics.recall_score(y_test, y_pred)*100,"%")
y_pred_prob = r.predict_proba(X_test)[:,1]
fp_rate, tp_rate, _ = metrics.roc_curve(y_test, y_pred_prob)
auc_score = metrics.roc_auc_score(y_test, y_pred_prob)
plt.rcParams['toolbar'] = 'None'
plt.title('Neural Network')
plt.xlabel('False Positive Rate')
plt.ylabel('True Positive Rate')
plt.plot(fp_rate,tp_rate,label="data 1, auc="+str(auc_score))
plt.legend(loc=4)
plt.show()
```

Output

```
File Edit Shell Debug Options Windows Help
Python 3.4.2 (default, Sep 26 2018, 07:16:01)
[GCC 4.9.2] on linux
Type "copyright", "credits" or "license()" for more information.
>>> ================================= RESTART =================================
>>>
K-Fold Classification Accuracy: 75.1182795699
[[21  6]
 [ 5 29]]
Confusion Matrix Accuracy: 81.9672131148 %
Confusion Matrix Precision: 82.8571428571 %
Confusion Matrix Recall: 85.2941176471 %
```
Ln: 6 Col: 0

FIGURE 4.17 Python Program MLP.py to Implement Neural Network Multi-layer Perceptron.

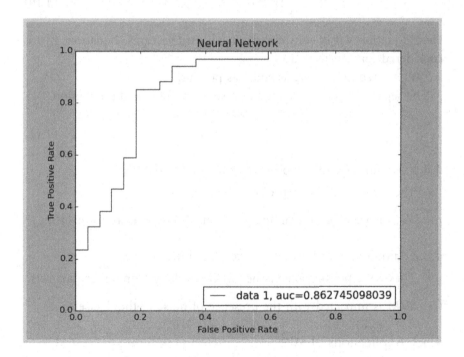

FIGURE 4.18   ROC Curve of Neural Network Multi-layer Perceptron.

4.8 SUPPORT VECTOR MACHINE

SVM is a supervised learning technique that helps in the classification and regression analysis of data. SVM strives to find a hyperplane that divides the data into corresponding classes. At the simplest level, a hyperplane is a straight line that divides the data into corresponding classes.

Support vectors are the data points nearest a hyperplane. The distance from the nearest data point to the hyperplane is known as a margin, and the goal is to have a wider margin for optimal classification.

The transformation of non-separable data points to transferable data points is possible through kernel functions.

In our discussion, let us consider the Linear SVM.

To get the maximum margin separation, the following Equations 4.9 and 4.10 need to be computed.

$$W^T X_i + b > +1 \tag{4.9}$$

$$W^T X_i + b < -1. \tag{4.10}$$

Here Equation 4.9 is considered for all positive cases. Equation 4.10 is considered for negative cases.

$\|W\|^2$ is required to be as small as possible.

The separator is then defined as a set of points for the Equation 4.11

$$W.x + b = 0. \tag{4.11}$$

4.8.1 Advantages of Support Vector Machines (SVM)

- They work well in high-dimensional spaces.

- SVM is capable of avoiding problems due to bias and overfitting.

4.8.2 Limitations of Support Vector Machines (SVM)

- They have performance issues when working with larger data sets.

- SVM is impacted with the presence of noise in the datasets.

4.8.3 Applications of SVM

- Image Classification

- Text Categorization

- Bioinformatics

Python program: svm.py

```
from pandas import read_csv
from sklearn.model_selection import KFold
from sklearn.svm import SVC
from sklearn.model_selection import cross_val_score
from sklearn.model_selection import train_test_split
from sklearn import metrics
from matplotlib import pyplot as plt
filename = 'heart.csv'
names = ['age','sex','cp','trestbps','chol','fbs','restecg','thalach','exang','old-
    peak','slope','ca','thal','target']
dataframe = read_csv(filename, names=names)
array = dataframe.values
X = array[:,0:13]
Y = array[:,13]
X_train, X_test, y_train, y_test = train_test_split(X, Y, test_size = 0.2,
    random_state = 0)
kfold = KFold(n_splits=10, random_state=7)
svmodel=SVC(kernel='linear',probability=True)
r=svmodel.fit(X_train, y_train)
results = cross_val_score(svmodel, X, Y, cv=kfold)
print("K-Fold Classification Accuracy:",results.mean()*100)
y_pred = svmodel.predict(X_test)
conf_matrix = metrics.confusion_matrix(y_test, y_pred)
print(conf_matrix)
print("Confusion Matrix Accuracy:",metrics.accuracy_score(y_test, y_pred)*
    100,"%")
print("Confusion Matrix Precision:",metrics.precision_score(y_test, y_pred)*
    100,"%")
print("Confusion Matrix Recall:",metrics.recall_score(y_test, y_pred)*100,"%")
y_pred_prob = r.predict_proba(X_test)[::,1]
fp_rate, tp_rate, _ = metrics.roc_curve(y_test, y_pred_prob)
auc_score = metrics.roc_auc_score(y_test, y_pred_prob)
plt.rcParams['toolbar'] = 'None'
plt.title('Support Vector Machine')
plt.xlabel('False Positive Rate')
plt.ylabel('True Positive Rate')
```

plt.plot(fp_rate,tp_rate,label="data 1, auc="+str(auc_score))
plt.legend(loc=4)
plt.show()

Output

```
File  Edit  Shell  Debug  Options  Windows  Help
Python 3.4.2 (default, Sep 26 2018, 07:16:01)
[GCC 4.9.2] on linux
Type "copyright", "credits" or "license()" for more information.
>>> ================================ RESTART ================================
>>>
K-Fold Classification Accuracy: 82.0860215054
[[20  7]
 [ 4 30]]
Confusion Matrix Accuracy: 81.9672131148 %
Confusion Matrix Precision: 81.0810810811 %
Confusion Matrix Recall: 88.2352941176 %
                                                                    Ln: 6 Col: 0
```

FIGURE 4.19   Python Program svm.py to Implement Support Vector Machine.

ROC Curve

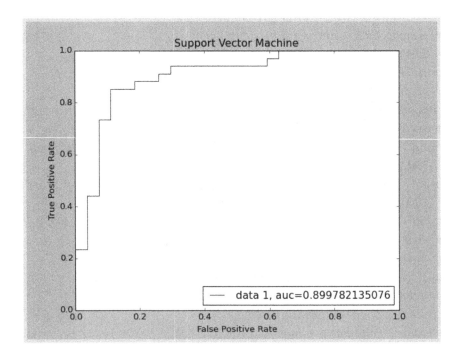

FIGURE 4.20   ROC Curve of Support Vector Machine.

4.9 RANDOM FOREST

Random forest falls under the category of supervised learning. Random forest builds multiple trees and merges them for an accurate decision. Thus, random forest is involved in building multiple decision trees.

4.9.1 Decision Tree

A Decision Tree follows a top-down approach in which the root nodes begin the process of binary splits with some criteria for the reduction in entropy. Here entropy is the measure of unpredictability in the data.

The root node N is the dataset with different class or labels of data. It is split into left and right subsets. The goal of these subsets is to have purity of class. If this is achieved at the corresponding node whose entropy is 0, only one kind of label is left. Otherwise, the process of splitting continues to determine the remaining labels.

Consider the dataset in Table 4.2

A simple decision process for illustrative purpose is shown in Figure 4.21.

4.9.2 Advantages of Random Forest

- The problem of overfitting is reduced.

- It has the capability to produce accurate predictions for large datasets.

- It has the ability to consider missing data.

TABLE 4.2   Mobile phone dataset

Color	Price	label
Gold	5000	iPhone
Blue	5000	Samsung
Black	3000	Nokia
Gold	5000	iPhone
Blue	5000	Samsung
Black	3000	Nokia

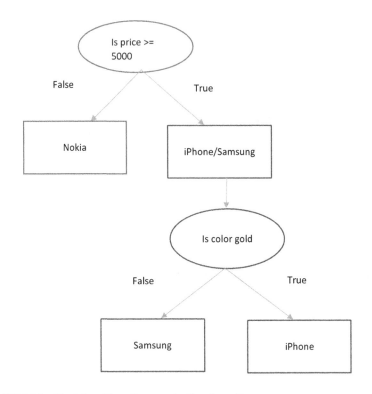

FIGURE 4.21 Decision Tree Process in Random Forest.

4.9.3 Limitations of Random Forest

- Trees are sensitive to data changes in the training data.

- A large number of trees can slow down the algorithm.

Python program: RandomForest.py
from pandas import read_csv
from sklearn.model_selection import KFold
from sklearn.preprocessing import StandardScaler
from sklearn.ensemble import RandomForestClassifier
from sklearn.model_selection import cross_val_score
from sklearn.model_selection import train_test_split
from sklearn import metrics

```
from matplotlib import pyplot as plt
filename = 'heart.csv'
names = ['age','sex','cp','trestbps','chol','fbs','restecg','thalach','exang','old-
    peak','slope','ca','thal','target']
dataframe = read_csv(filename, names=names)
array = dataframe.values
X = array[:,0:13]
Y = array[:,13]
X_train, X_test, y_train, y_test = train_test_split(X, Y, test_size = 0.2,
    random_state = 0)
kfold = KFold(n_splits=10, random_state=7)
stdc = StandardScaler()
X_train = stdc.fit_transform(X_train)
X_test = stdc.transform(X_test)
clf = RandomForestClassifier()
r=clf.fit(X_train, y_train)
results = cross_val_score(clf, X, Y, cv=kfold)
print("K-Fold Classification Accuracy:",results.mean()*100)
y_pred = clf.predict(X_test)
conf_matrix = metrics.confusion_matrix(y_test, y_pred)
print(conf_matrix)
print("Confusion Matrix Accuracy:",metrics.accuracy_score(y_test, y_pred)*
    100,"%")
print("Confusion Matrix Precision:",metrics.precision_score(y_test, y_pred)*
    100,"%")
print("Confusion Matrix Recall:",metrics.recall_score(y_test, y_pred)*100,"%")
y_pred_prob = r.predict_proba(X_test)[:,1]
fp_rate, tp_rate, _ = metrics.roc_curve(y_test, y_pred_prob)
auc_score = metrics.roc_auc_score(y_test, y_pred_prob)
plt.rcParams['toolbar'] = 'None'
plt.title('Random Forest')
plt.xlabel('False Positive Rate')
plt.ylabel('True Positive Rate')
plt.plot(fp_rate,tp_rate,label="data 1, auc="+str(auc_score))
plt.legend(loc=4)
plt.show()
```

Output

```
File  Edit  Shell  Debug  Options  Windows  Help
Python 3.4.2 (default, Sep 26 2018, 07:16:01)
[GCC 4.9.2] on linux
Type "copyright", "credits" or "license()" for more information.
>>> ================================ RESTART ================================
>>>
K-Fold Classification Accuracy: 78.1935483871
[[24  3]
 [ 6 28]]
Confusion Matrix Accuracy: 85.2459016393 %
Confusion Matrix Precision: 90.3225806452 %
Confusion Matrix Recall: 82.3529411765 %
```
Ln: 6 Col: 0

FIGURE 4.22   Python Program RandomForest.py to Implement Random Forest.

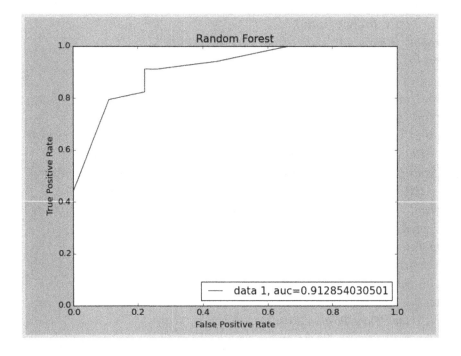

FIGURE 4.23   ROC Curve of Random Forest.

4.10 K NEIGHBORS

K Neighbors (also known as K Nearest Neighbors (KNN)) is a supervised learning algorithm. In this type of instance-based learning, the training observations are retained as the part of the model. It is known as competition-based learning because it uses competition between data instances for prediction. It is also called lazy learning because the decision to build a model is pushed until the time for prediction. When KNN is referred as non-parametric, it means that it makes no assumptions of the underlying data distributions.

K nearest neighbors are employed perform classification. Euclidean distance formula is used to measure the distance as in Equation 4.12

$$d(a, b) = \sum_{i=1}^{n} (b_i - a_i)^2. \tag{4.12}$$

The Euclidean distance between the two points provides the length of the path connecting them.

KNN believes that samples with similar inputs belong to the same class as illustrated in Figure 4.24(a) and Figure 4.24(b).

Here ? is the new sample and + and – stand for training data samples

The value of k determines the closest neighbors to consider. When K=1, the label of the new sample will be that of the 1 closest neighbor.

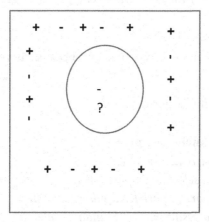

FIGURE 4.24 A   K= 1 in KNN.

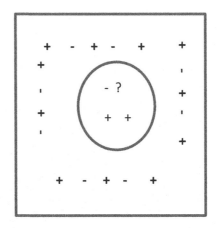

FIGURE 4.24 B   K= 3 in KNN.

When K=3 a voting by majority is considered. Suppose if two labels are X and one label is Y. Then, per the majority system, the new label will be X. In a tie, then a tie-breaker rule (e.g., closest neighbor label or random label) is chosen.

4.10.1 Advantages of KNN

- KNN is relatively fast for small training data sets.

- It makes no assumption of data and works well for non-linear data.

- It can be applied for both classification and regression.

4.10.2 Limitations of KNN

- KNN is computationally expensive because it retains the training data.

- It is sensitive for larger datasets.

Python program: kneighbor.py
from pandas import read_csv
from sklearn.model_selection import KFold
from sklearn.neighbors import KNeighborsClassifier
from sklearn.preprocessing import StandardScaler
from sklearn.model_selection import cross_val_score

```
from sklearn.model_selection import train_test_split
from sklearn import metrics
from matplotlib import pyplot as plt
filename = 'heart.csv'
names    = ['age','sex','cp','trestbps','chol','fbs','restecg','thalach','exang','old-
    peak','slope','ca','thal','target']
dataframe = read_csv(filename, names=names)
array = dataframe.values
X = array[:,0:13]
Y = array[:,13]
X_train, X_test, y_train, y_test = train_test_split(X,Y,test_size=0.2,random_
    state=0)
kfold = KFold(n_splits=10, random_state=7)
ksc = StandardScaler()
ksc.fit(X_train)
X_train = ksc.transform(X_train)
X_test = ksc.transform(X_test)
knclf = KNeighborsClassifier(n_neighbors=5)
r=knclf.fit(X_train, y_train)
results = cross_val_score(knclf, X, Y, cv=kfold)
print("K-Fold Classification Accuracy:",results.mean()*100)
y_pred = knclf.predict(X_test)
conf_matrix = metrics.confusion_matrix(y_test, y_pred)
print("The Confusion Matrix is: ")
print(conf_matrix)
print("Confusion Matrix Accuracy:",metrics.accuracy_score(y_test, y_pred)*
    100,"%")
print("Confusion Matrix Precision:",metrics.precision_score(y_test, y_pred)*
    100,"%")
print("Confusion Matrix Recall:",metrics.recall_score(y_test, y_pred)*100,"%")
y_pred_prob = r.predict_proba(X_test)[:,1]
fp_rate, tp_rate, _ = metrics.roc_curve(y_test, y_pred_prob)
auc_score = metrics.roc_auc_score(y_test, y_pred_prob)
plt.rcParams['toolbar'] = 'None'
plt.title('K Nearest Neighbor')
plt.xlabel('False Positive Rate')
plt.ylabel('True Positive Rate')
```

plt.plot(fp_rate,tp_rate,label="data 1, auc="+str(auc_score))
plt.legend(loc=4)
plt.show()

Output

```
File  Edit  Shell  Debug  Options  Windows  Help
Python 3.4.2 (default, Sep 26 2018, 07:16:01)
[GCC 4.9.2] on linux
Type "copyright", "credits" or "license()" for more information.
>>> ================================ RESTART ================================
>>>
K-Fold Classification Accuracy: 55.4301075269
The Confusion Matrix is:
[[21  6]
 [ 5 29]]
Confusion Matrix Accuracy: 81.9672131148 %
Confusion Matrix Precision: 82.8571428571 %
Confusion Matrix Recall: 85.2941176471 %

                                                                 Ln: 6 Col: 0
```

FIGURE 4.25   Python Program kneighbor.py to Implement K Neighbors.

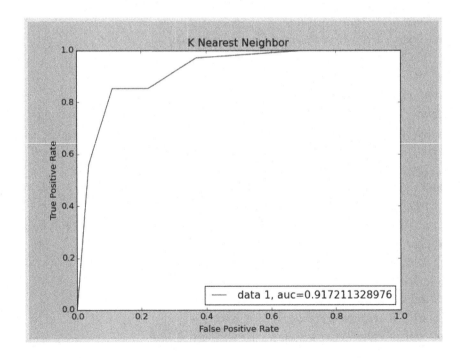

FIGURE 4.26   ROC Curve of K Neighbors.

4.11 LINEAR DISCRIMINANT ANALYSIS (LDA)

Linear Discriminant Analysis (LDA) is a supervised learning technique. It is used as a dimensionality reduction technique. LDA as a classification technique was developed by R. A. Fisher.

LDA tries to achieve

- Making the distance between the two clusters large.

- Making the intra-cluster distance small.

Select "W" to maximize the ratio of between-class scatter and the within-class scatter.

The between class scatter matrix is defined in Equation 4.13

$$S_B = \sum_{i=1}^{c} N_i (\mu_i - \mu)(\mu_i - \mu)^T, \qquad (4.13)$$

where μ_i is the mean of the class X_i

N_i is the number of samples in class

$X_i \mu$ is the overall mean of the data

c is the overall number of classes.

The within-class scatter matrix is

$$S_W = \sum_{i=1}^{c} \cdot \sum_{x_k \in x_i} (x_k - \mu_i)(x_k - u_i)^T, \qquad (4.14)$$

here x_k is the subset of the sample class X_i

The generalized eigenvalue problem of the matrix is given in Equation 4.15

$$S_w^{-1} S_B. \qquad (4.15)$$

Equation 4.15 is solved to compute w Eigenvectors that maximize Equation 4.16

$$w = \arg \max \left| \frac{W^T S_B W}{W^T S_W W} \right|. \qquad (4.16)$$

Sort the eigenvectors by decreasing eigenvalues and choose the k eigenvectors with the largest eigenvalues to form a transformation matrix. Use the transformation matrix to convert the original data set to lower dimension space.

4.11.1 Advantages of LDA

- LDA is simple and mathematically robust.

- It produces results with accuracy comparable with more complex models.

4.11.2 Limitations of LDA

- LDA is sensitive to overfitting.

- It is not well suited to non-linear problems.

Python program: LDA.py

```
from pandas import read_csv
from sklearn.model_selection import KFold
from sklearn.discriminant_analysis import LinearDiscriminantAnalysis
from sklearn.preprocessing import StandardScaler
from sklearn.model_selection import cross_val_score
from sklearn.model_selection import train_test_split
from sklearn import metrics
from matplotlib import pyplot as plt
filename = 'heart.csv'
names = ['age','sex','cp','trestbps','chol','fbs','restecg','thalach','exang','old-peak','slope','ca','thal','target']
dataframe = read_csv(filename, names=names)
array = dataframe.values
X = array[:,0:13]
Y = array[:,13]
X_train, X_test, y_train, y_test = train_test_split(X,Y,test_size=0.2, random_state=0)
kfold = KFold(n_splits=10, random_state=7)
lsc = StandardScaler()
lsc.fit(X_train)
X_train = lsc.transform(X_train)
```

```
X_test = lsc.transform(X_test)
ldac = LinearDiscriminantAnalysis()
r = ldac.fit_transform(X_train, y_train)
results = cross_val_score(ldac, X, Y, cv=kfold)
print("K-Fold Classification Accuracy:",results.mean()*100)
y_pred = ldac.predict(X_test)
conf_matrix = metrics.confusion_matrix(y_test, y_pred)
print("The Confusion Matrix is: ")
print(conf_matrix)
print("Confusion Matrix Accuracy:",metrics.accuracy_score(y_test, y_pred)*
    100,"%")
print("Confusion Matrix Precision:",metrics.precision_score(y_test, y_pred)*
    100,"%")
print("Confusion Matrix Recall:",metrics.recall_score(y_test, y_pred)*100,"%")
y_pred_prob = ldac.predict_proba(X_test)[::,1]
fp_rate, tp_rate, _ = metrics.roc_curve(y_test, y_pred_prob)
auc_score = metrics.roc_auc_score(y_test, y_pred_prob)
plt.rcParams['toolbar'] = 'None'
plt.title('Linear Discriminant Analysis')
plt.xlabel('False Positive Rate')
plt.ylabel('True Positive Rate')
plt.plot(fp_rate,tp_rate,label="data 1, auc="+str(auc_score))
plt.legend(loc=4)
plt.show()
```

Output

```
File Edit Shell Debug Options Windows Help
Python 3.4.2 (default, Sep 26 2018, 07:16:01)
[GCC 4.9.2] on linux
Type "copyright", "credits" or "license()" for more information.
>>> ============================== RESTART ==============================
>>>
K-Fold Classification Accuracy: 80.7634408602
The Confusion Matrix is:
[[20  7]
 [ 3 31]]
Confusion Matrix Accuracy: 83.606557377 %
Confusion Matrix Precision: 81.5789473684 %
Confusion Matrix Recall: 91.1764705882 %
                                                                    Ln: 6 Col: 0
```

FIGURE 4.27   Python Program LDA.py to Implement Linear Discriminant Analysis.

ROC Curve

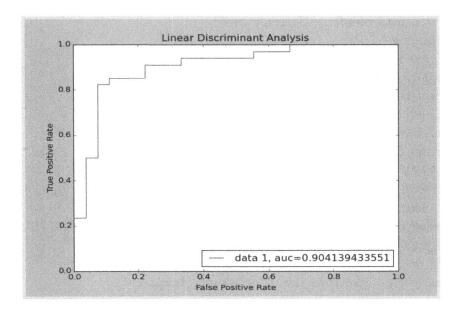

FIGURE 4.28   ROC Curve of Linear Discriminant Analysis.

EXERCISES

I. Answer the following briefly.

1. Define Machine Learning.

2. Bring out the difference between Supervised and Unsupervised Learning.

3. What is meant by Reinforcement Learning?

4. What is the difference between classification and regression?

5. List the metrics for classification.

6. What is a CSV file; which Pandas function do you use to load it?

7. What is the advantage of drawing the correlation of data?

8. Is it good to use Logistic Regression for classification or as the name suggests for regression?

9. Does the Neural Network mimic the function of the human brain? Justify briefly.

10. Give the application areas in which Naive Bayes could be applied.

11. What is meant by overfitting?

12. What is the role of the sigmoid function?

13. Can SVMs be applied to regression also?

14. Does Random Forest depend on decision trees?

15. Is K Nearest Neighbor Supervised or Unsupervised learning?

16. Who developed the Linear Discriminant Analysis technique?

II. Using the Prima Indians diabetes dataset, apply the following supervised machine learning algorithms:

- Logistic Regression
- Naïve Bayes
- Neural Network
- SVM
- Random Forest
- K N N
- LDA

Download Prima Indians diabetes dataset from http://networkrepository.com/pima-indians-diabetes.php

Compare the results of classification metrics of the best performing and worst performing algorithms and justify the reasons for their good and poor performances.

## CHAPTER 5

Introduction to Image Processing

I mage processing is a technique for performing a specific operation to an image, in order to produce an enriched image or to obtain some useful information from it. Digital image processing is rapidly growing in the field of computer science; it plays an important role in science and technology, with applications in the fields of photography, television, remote sensing, robotics, industrial inspection and medical diagnosis.

Image-Processing Applications

- Computerized Photography (e.g., Photoshop)

- Fingerprint/face/iris Recognition

- Space-Image Processing (e.g., interplanetary probe images, Hubble space telescope images)

- Automatic Character Recognition (e.g., license-plate recognition)

- Medical/biological Image Processing (e.g., interpretation of X-ray images, blood/cellular microscopic images)

- Industrial Applications (e.g., product inspection/sorting)

In the following report, image-processing operations will be implemented using the Raspberry Pi. Raspberry Pi is based on python and OpenCV packages.

In this we chapter, we show how to:

- Load, display and save images on Raspberry Pi.

- Scale (resize) images.

- Vary the brightness of images.

- Perform bitwise operations.

- Blur and sharpen images.

- Perform thresholding on images.

- Perform erosion and dilation.

- Perform edge detection on images.

- Perform image segmentation.

5.1 LOAD, DISPLAY AND SAVE AN IMAGE ON RASPBERRY PI, USING PYTHON AND OPEN CV

```
# Import Computer Vision package – cv2
import cv2

# Read the image using imread built-in function
image = cv2.imread('image_1.jpg')

# Display original image using imshow built-in function
cv2.imshow("Original", image)

# Wait until any key is pressed
cv2.waitKey(0)

# Save the image using imwrite built-in function
cv2.imwrite("Saved Image.jpg", image)
```

Output:

FIGURE 5.1   Output of Python Program Load, Display and Save an Image on Raspberry Pi.

- The objective of this code is to load, display and save an image. The first step is to import the computer vision package *cv2*.

- We can read the image using the built-in function, **cv2.imread**. The **cv2.imread** function takes one parameter within a single inverted quote, which is. the name of the image.

- We can display the image using the built-in function, **cv2.imshow**. The **cv2.imshow** function requires 2 parameters: the name under which the image is saved and the variable containing the read image.

- To save the image, we can use the built-in function, **cv2.imwrite**.

- The built-in function, **cv2.waitkey**, is used to wait until you press any key in the keyboard.

5.2 SCALING (RESIZING) IMAGES – CUBIC, AREA AND LINEAR INTERPOLATIONS

Python Program: Scaling.py

```
import cv2
import numpy as np
image = cv2.imread('image_2.jpg')
cv2.imshow("Original", image)
cv2.waitKey()
# cv2.resize(image, output image size, x scale, y scale, interpolation)
# Scaling using cubic interpolation
scaling_cubic = cv2.resize(image, None, fx=.75, fy=.75, interpolation =
    cv2.INTER_CUBIC)
cv2.imshow('Cubic Interpolated', scaling_cubic)
cv2.waitKey()
# Scaling using area interpolation
scaling_skewed = cv2.resize(image, (600, 300), interpolation = cv2.
    INTER_AREA)
cv2.imshow('Area Interpolated', scaling_skewed)
cv2.waitKey()
scaling_linear = cv2.resize(image, None, fx=0.5, fy=0.5, interpolation =
    cv2.INTER_LINEAR)
# Scaling using linear interpolation
cv2.imshow('Linear Interpolated', scaling_linear)
cv2.waitKey()
cv2.destroyAllWindows()
```

Output:

FIGURE 5.2   Output of Python Program to Display Original Image.

FIGURE 5.3   Output of Python Program to Display Scaling Using Cubic Interpolation.

FIGURE 5.4 Output of Python Program Load to Display Scaling Using Area Interpolation.

FIGURE 5.5 Output of Python Program Load to Display Scaling Using Linear Interpolation.

- This program involves image scaling to resize the image.

- OpenCV utilizes the function **cv2.resize()** for this purpose. The size of the image can be specified either manually or with the scaling factor. There are different interpolation methods, preferably **cv2.**

INTER_AREA for shrinking the image and **cv2.INTER_CUBIC** (slow) and **cv2.INTER_LINEAR** for enlarging the image. The default interpolation method used is **cv2.INTER_LINEAR** for all resizing purposes.

- **cv2.resize(image, output image size, x scale, y scale, interpolation)**

This function takes five parameters. The first parameter is the name of the image to be resized, the second parameter is the size of the output image, the third and fourth parameters are the scaling factors of the image in both the x- and y-axis and the final parameter specifies the interpolation to be used, namely cubic, area, or linear. The default interpolation is linear. All interpolation methods take the dimensions of the output image and the image's scaling factor as parameters.

- **cv2.INTER_CUBIC** is the command for cubic interpolation, **cv2. INTER_AREA** for area interpolation and **cv2.INTER_LINEAR** for linear interpolation.

- The built-in function **cv2.destroyAllWindow()** closes all windows once any key is pressed.

5.3 VARYING BRIGHTNESS OF IMAGES USING ADD AND SUBTRACT OPERATIONS

Python Program: Varying_Brightness.py

```
import cv2
import numpy as np
image = cv2.imread('image_4.jpg')
cv2.imshow("Original", image)
cv2.waitKey(0)
# np.ones returns an array of given shape and type, filled with ones
# np.ones(shape, dtype)
matrix = np.ones(image.shape, dtype = "uint8") * 120
```

```
# image.shape: gives takes the shape of original image
# uint8: unsigned integer (0 to 255)
# matrix: contains ones, having same dimension as original image but
    mutlipied by 120
# Adding matrix to orginal image increases brightness
add = cv2.add(image, matrix)
cv2.imshow("Added", add)
cv2.waitKey(0)
# Subtracting matrix from original image decreases brightness
subtract = cv2.subtract(image, matrix)
cv2.imshow("Subtracted", subtract)
cv2.waitKey(0)
cv2.destroyAllWindows()
```

Output:

FIGURE 5.6   Output of Python Program to Display Original Image.

FIGURE 5.7 Output of Python Program That Adds Matrix to Original Image to Increase Brightness.

FIGURE 5.8 Output of Python Program That Subtracts Matrix to Original Image to Increase Brightness.

- This program varies the brightness of the image, using addition, subtraction and arithmetic operations.

- The function **np.ones** returns an array consisting entirely of ones, based on the given inputs of shape and type. In this example, we used the data type uint8: unsigned integer (0 to 255). This array matrix consists of ones, having the same dimensions as the original image, multiplied by 120.

- The built-in function **cv2.add(image, matrix)** is applied to add the array matrix **np.ones** to the original image in order to increase the brightness.

- The built-in function **cv2.subtract(image, matrix)** subtracts the array matrix **np.ones** from the original image in order to decrease the brightness.

5.4 BITWISE OPERATIONS – AND, OR, XOR, NOT

Python Program: Bitwise_Operations.py
```
import cv2
import numpy as np
# np.zeros(shape, dtype)
rectangle = np.zeros((200, 200), np.uint8)
# dimension of the rectangle is 200 x 200
# uint8: is an unsigned integer (0 to 255)

# Creating rectangle using cv2.rectangle built-in function
# cv2.rectangle(image, (x1,y1), (x2,y2), color, thickness)
cv2.rectangle(rectangle, (20, 20), (180, 180), 255, -1)
cv2.imshow("Rect", rectangle)
cv2.waitKey(0)
# np.zeros(shape, dtype)
circle = np.zeros((200, 200), dtype = "uint8")
```

```
# dimension of the circle is 200 x 200
# uint8: is an unsigned integer (0 to 255)

# Creating circle using cv2.circle built-in function
# cv2.circle(image, centre, radius, color, thickness)
cv2.circle(circle, (100, 100), 100, 255, -1)
cv2.imshow("Circle", circle)
cv2.waitKey(0)
# Performing bitwise AND operation on rectangle, circle
# cv2.bitwise_and(src1, src2)
And = cv2.bitwise_and(rectangle, circle)
# AND operation
# A B Output
# 0 0 0
# 0 1 0
# 1 0 0
# 1 1 1
cv2.imshow("AND", And)
cv2.waitKey(0)
# Performing bitwise OR operation on rectangle, circle
# cv2.bitwise_or(src1, src2)
Or = cv2.bitwise_or(rectangle, circle)
# OR operation
# A B Output
# 0 0 0
# 0 1 1
# 1 0 1
# 1 1 1
cv2.imshow("OR", Or)
cv2.waitKey(0)
# Performing bitwise XOR operation on rectangle, circle
```

```
# cv2.bitwise_xor(src1, src2)
Xor = cv2.bitwise_xor(rectangle, circle)
# XOR operation
# A B Output
# 0 0 0
# 0 1 1
# 1 0 1
# 1 1 0
cv2.imshow("XOR", Xor)
cv2.waitKey(0)
# Performing bitwise NOT operation on rectangle
# cv2.bitwise_not(src1)
Not_rect = cv2.bitwise_not(rectangle)
# NOT operation
# A Output
# 0 1
# 1 0
cv2.imshow("NOT1", Not_rect)
cv2.waitKey(0)
# Performing bitwise NOT operation on circle
# cv2.bitwise_not(src1)
Not_circ = cv2.bitwise_not(circle)
# NOT operation
# A Output
# 0 1
# 1 0
cv2.imshow("NOT2", Not_circ)
cv2.waitKey(0)
cv2.destroyAllWindows()
```

Output:

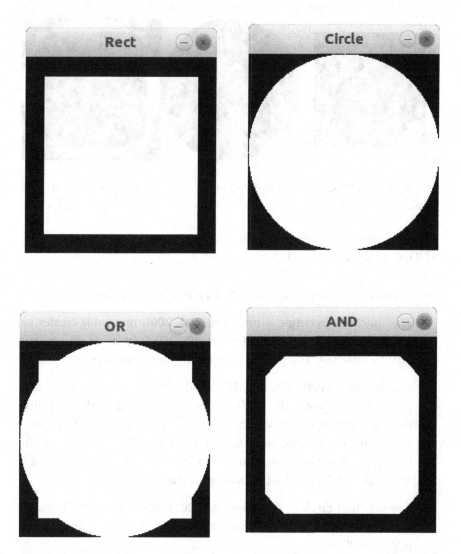

FIGURE 5.9 Output of Python Program to Display Rectangle, Circle, OR and AND Operations.

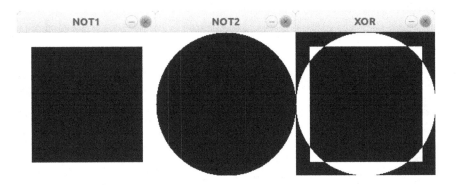

FIGURE 5.10 Output of Python Program to Display NOT, NOT1 and XOR Operations.

This program performs bit-wise operations and uses the operations AND, OR, XOR and NOT.

- Initially, two shapes are created: a rectangle and a circle.

- The function **rectangle = np.zeros((200, 200), np.uint8)** creates an array of zeroes, with dimensions of 200*200 (any other dimensions may be inputted) and data type np.unit8 (unsigned integer of 8bits).

- **cv2.rectangle(rectangle, (20, 20), (180, 180), 255, -1):** The rectangle is created using the built-in function **cv2.rectangle.** The first input parameter is the "variable" (in this case, "rectangle"), the next inputs are the coordinates (X1,Y1) and (X2, Y2), followed by the color, which varies from 0 to 255, with 255 returning white and 0 returning black; the final parameter is the thickness.

- The function **circle = np.zeros((200, 200), dtype = "uint8")** creates an array of zeroes with dimension of 200*200 and data type unsigned integer of 8 bits.

- **cv2.circle(circle, (100, 100), 100, 255, -1):** Similarly to the rectangle, the circle is created using the built-in function **cv2.circle,** which has the input parameters "variable name" (in this case, "circle"), "center of the circle location", "radius", "color" (0 to 255) and "thickness".

- Bitwise operations are performed on the resulting two images, rectangle and circle:

- The "AND" operation is performed using the built-in function **cv2. bitwise_and**; the "OR" operation is performed using the built-in function **cv2.bitwise_or**; the "XOR" operation is performed using the built-in function **cv2.bitwise_xor**; the "NOT" operation is performed with the built-in function **cv2.bitwise_not**. All four functions use the input parameters of the two shapes (rectangle and circle).

5.5 BLURRING AND SHARPENING IMAGES

Python Program:Blurring_Sharpening.py

```
import cv2
import numpy as np
image = cv2.imread('image_5.jpg')
cv2.imshow("Original", image)
cv2.waitKey(0)
# Blurring images: Averaging, cv2.blur built-in function
# Averaging: Convolving image with normalized box filter
# Convolution: Mathematical operation on 2 functions which produces
    third function.
# Normalized box filter having size 3 x 3 would be:
# (1/9) [[1, 1, 1],
#              [1, 1, 1],
#              [1, 1, 1]]
blur = cv2.blur(image,(9,9)) # (9 x 9) filter is used
cv2.imshow('Blurred', blur)
cv2.waitKey(0)
# Sharpening images: Emphasizes edges in an image
kernel = np.array([[-1,-1,-1],
        [-1,9,-1],
        [-1,-1,-1]])
# If we don't normalize to 1, image will be brighter or darker, respectively

# cv2.filter2D is the built-in function used for sharpening images
# cv2.filter2D(image, ddepth, kernel)
sharpened = cv2.filter2D(image, -1, kernel)
# ddepth = -1, sharpened images will have same depth as original image
cv2.imshow('Sharpened', sharpened)
cv2.waitKey(0)
cv2.destroyAllWindows()
```

Output:

FIGURE 5.11   Output of Python Program to Display Original Image.

FIGURE 5.12   Output of Python Program to Display Blurred Image.

FIGURE 5.13   Output of Python Program to Display Sharpened Image.

- This program blurs and sharpens the image.

- The built-in function **cv2.blur** blurs the image, using a concept called averaging. Averaging applies the mathematical process of convolution to the image with a normalized box filter. Convolution is a mathematical operation describing how one function may alter another to produce a third function.

- For example, if you consider a normalized box filter with dimensions of 4*4 (i.e., 4 rows and 4 columns, with each element equal to 1), the total value equals 16, so we will multiply it by 1/16. Here we used the read image and a (9*9) normalized box filter as the input parameters.

- The built-in function **cv2.filter2D** sharpens the image by emphasizing the edges. There are three input parameters required: first is the read image, second is the depth (if we input a depth of -1, the sharpened image will have the same depth as the original image) and the third variable is the kernel.

5.6 THRESHOLDING – BINARY THRESHOLDING

Python Program:Thresholding.py

```
import cv2
import numpy as np
image = cv2.imread('image_6.jpg')
cv2.imshow("Original", image)
cv2.waitKey(0)
# cv2.COLOR_BGR2GRAY: Converts color(RGB) image to gray
# BGR(bytes are reversed)
# cv2.cvtColor: Converts image from one color space to another
gray = cv2.cvtColor(image, cv2.COLOR_BGR2GRAY)
# cv2.threshold built-in function which performs thresholding
# cv2.threshold(image, threshold_value, max_value, threshold_type)
ret,threshold = cv2.threshold(gray, 127, 255, cv2.THRESH_BINARY)
cv2.imshow('Binary Thresholding', threshold)
cv2.waitKey(0)
cv2.destroyAllWindows()
```

Output:

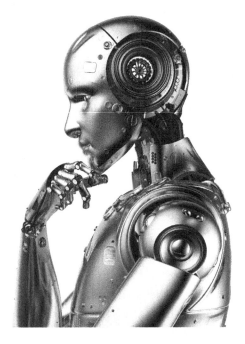

FIGURE 5.14 Output of Python Program to Display Original Image.

FIGURE 5.15   Output of Python Program to Display Binary Threshold Image.

- This program utilizes thresholding to convert a grayscale image into binary.

- If there is a color image, it must first be converted into grayscale before applying thresholding, so it can be converted to binary.

- To convert a color image to grayscale, we use the built-in function **cv2.cvtColor(image, cv2.COLOR_BGR2GRAY)**.

- "BGR2GRAY", describes the conversion of the primary colors RGB (red, green, and blue) into gray, stated conversely as BGR (blue, green, red) because the bites are saved in reverse order.

- The built-in function **cv2.Color** converts from one color space to another, i.e. from color to grayscale.

- The built-in function **cv2.threshold** applies binary thresholding.

- *ret,threshold = cv2.threshold(gray, 127, 255, cv2.THRESH_BINARY):* This function converts the image from color to gray, utilizing the variable "gray" that we have saved after the BGR2GRAY conversion. Using the threshold value from 0 to 255 (based on 8 bits), we can modify the image brightness before using the thresholding type, **cv2. THRESH_BINARY.**

5.7 MORPHOLOGICAL OPERATIONS: EROSION AND DILATION

```
import cv2
import numpy as np
image = cv2.imread('image_7.jpg')
cv2.imshow("Original", image)
cv2.waitKey(0)
# np.ones returns an array, given shape and type, filled with ones
# np.ones(shape, dtype)
kernel = np.ones((5,5), dtype = "uint8")
# 5 x 5 is the dimension of the kernel
# uint8: is an unsigned integer (0 to 255)

# cv2.erode is the built-in function used for erosion
# cv2.erode(image, kernel, iterations)
erosion = cv2.erode(image, kernel, iterations = 1)
cv2.imshow("Erosion", erosion)
cv2.waitKey(0)
# cv2.dilate is the built-in function used for dilation
# cv2.dilate(image, kernel, iterations)
dilation = cv2.dilate(image, kernel, iterations = 1)
cv2.imshow("Dilation", dilation)
cv2.waitKey(0)
cv2.destroyAllWindows()
```

Output:

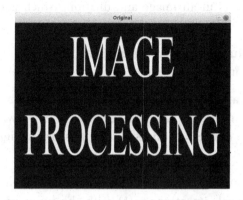

FIGURE 5.16　Output of Python Program to Display Original Image.

FIGURE 5.17　Output of Python Program to Display Eroded Image.

FIGURE 5.18　Output of Python Program to Display Dilated Image.

- This program applies erosion, which removes pixels at the boundaries of objects in an image and dilation, which adds pixels to the boundaries of objects in an image.

- **np.ones** returns an array of a given shape and type, consisting entirely of ones.

- **np.ones(shape, dtype)**: Here we use the variable "kernel" and assign np.ones(5,5), with dimension of 5*5, with format **np. ones((5,5), dtype = "uint8")**. uint8 is an unsigned integer of 8 bits.

- With the built-in erosion function, **cv2.erode**, we use **cv2.erode (image, kernel, iterations = 1)** with the input parameters of the image, the kernel and the number of iterations.

- With the built-in dilation function, cv2.dilate, the format is **cv2. dilate(image, kernel, iterations = 1)**, using the same inputs of image, kernel, and iterations.

5.8 EDGE DETECTION USING CANNY EDGE DETECTOR

```
import cv2
import numpy as np
image = cv2.imread('image_8.jpg')
cv2.imshow("Original", image)
cv2.waitKey(0)
# cv2.Canny is the built-in function used to detect edges
# cv2.Canny(image, threshold_1, threshold_2)
canny = cv2.Canny(image, 50, 200)
cv2.imshow('Canny Edge Detection', canny)
cv2.waitKey(0)
cv2. destroyAllWindows()
```

Output:

FIGURE 5.19   Output of Python Program to Display Original Image.

FIGURE 5.20   Output of Python Program to Demonstrate Canny Edge Detection.

- This program detects edges within the image.
- We use canny edge detector, generally considered the most powerful and efficient approach; it is therefore the most commonly used in many real-time applications.

- We use the built-in function **cv2.Canny(image, 50, 200)**, which requires three input parameters: the image with which we are working, the lower-limit, threshold_1 and the upper limit, threshold_2.

5.9 IMAGE SEGMENTATION USING CONTOURS

```
# Segmentation: Partitioning images into different regions
# Contours: Lines or curves around the boundary of an object
import cv2
import numpy as np
image = cv2.imread('image_9.jpg')
cv2.imshow("Original", image)
cv2.waitKey(0)
# cv2.Canny is the built-in function used to detect edges
# cv2.Canny(image, threshold_1, threshold_2)
canny = cv2.Canny(image, 50, 200)
cv2.imshow("Canny Edge Detection", canny)
cv2.waitKey(0)
# cv2.findContours is the built-in function to find contours
# cv2.findContours(canny, contour retrieval mode, contour approximation
    mode)
# contour retrieval mode: cv2.RETR_LIST (retrieves all contours)
# contour approximation mode: cv2.CHAIN_APPROX_NONE (stores all
    boundary points)
contours,hierarchy=cv2.findContours(canny,cv2.RETR_LIST,cv2.
    CHAIN_APPROX_NONE)
# cv2.drawContours is the the built-in function to draw contours
# cv2.drawContours(image, contours, index of contours, color, thickness
cv2.drawContours(image, contours, -1, (255,0,0), 10)
# index of contours = -1 will draw all the contours
cv2.imshow("Contours", image)
cv2.waitKey()
cv2.destroyAllWindows()
```

Output:

FIGURE 5.21   Output of Python Program to Display Original Image.

FIGURE 5.22   Output of Python Program to Display Image Contours.

- This program performs image segmentation, which partitions the image into different regions, using contours, which are the lines or curves around the boundary of an object.

- We use canny edge detection to find the contours, with the built-in function. **cv2.findContours**.

- **cv2.findContours(canny, contour retrieval mode, contour approximation mode):**

- Contour retrieval mode: **cv2.RETR_LIST** (retrieves all contours).

- Contour approximation mode: **cv2.CHAIN_APPROX_NONE** (stores all boundary points).

- **cv2.drawContours** is the built-in function to draw contours.

- **cv2.drawContours(image, contours, index of contours, color, thickness):** inputting index of contours and a thickness of −1 draws all contours.

Bibliography

[1]. Derek Molloy, *Exploring Raspberry Pi: Interfacing to the Real World with Embedded Linux*, Wiley Publication,United States, 2016.

[2]. Steven Lawrence Fernandes, *Raspberry Pi 3 Cookbook for Python Programmers: Unleash the Potential of Raspberry Pi 3 with Over 100 Recipes*, 3rd Edition, Packt Publications, United Kingdom, 2018.

[3]. Leonard Eddison, *Raspberry Pi: A Step by Step Guide for Beginners*, CreateSpace Independent Publishing Platform, 2018.

[4]. Claus Fuhrer, Jan Erik Solem and Olivier Verdier, *Scientific Computing with Python 3*, Packt Publications, United Kingdom, 2016.

[5]. Shrirang Ambaji Kulkarni, *Problem Solving and Python Programming*, yesdee Publications, India, 2019.

[6]. Andreas C. Müller and Sarah Guido, *Introduction to Machine Learning with Python: A Guide for Data Scientists*, 1st Edition, O'Reilly Publication, United States, 2016.

[7]. Sebastian Raschka, *Python Machine Learning*, Packt Publications, United Kingdom, 2015.

[8]. Peter Harrington, *Machine Learning in Action*, Manning Publication, 2012.

Index

Page numbers in *italics* refer to Figures, and page numbers in **bold** refer to Tables.

A

Area interpolation, 128–131, *130*
ARM (Advanced RISC Machines), 7
Arrays, *See also* Matrices
    attributes, 41–42, **42**, *42*
    concatenation, 47–49, *47*, *48*, *49*
    copying, 46, *46*
    creating
        with 0s, 38–39, *39*
        with 1s of Integar64 type, 41, *41*
        from a Python list, 37–38, *37*, *38*
        with random values, 40–41, *40*, *41*
        with values 0 to, 9, 39, *39*
    indexing and access, 43, *43*
    reshaping, 46, *47*
    splitting, 49–50, *49*, *50*
    subarrays
        1-Dimensional array, 44, *44*
        2-Dimensional array, 45–46,
        45, *46*
Artificial Neural Network *See* Neural
    network MLP
Audio jack, 10, *11*

B

Big data, 4
Binary thresholding images, 142–144,
    142, *143*
Bitwise operations, 134–139, *137*, *138*
BlueJ, 14
Bluetooth, 12

Blurring

Blurring and sharpening images, 139–141,
    140, *141*
Brightness adjustment, 131–134, *132*, *133*

C

Canny edge detection (images),
    146–148, *147*
Cholesky decomposition, 70, *71*
Classification in machine learning, 82–83
    metrics
        confusion (error) matrix, 84–85,
        84, 95
        k-fold cross-validation, 83
    models, 91–95
Confusion (error) matrix, 84–85, *84*, 95
Contours, image segmentation using,
    148–150, *149*
Correlation, 89
Covariance matrix, 89–90, *89*, *90*
Cross-validation *See* K-fold cross-
    validation
CSV (comma separated value) files, reading
    Pandas, 63, *63*
    Scikit-Learn, 85, *87*, 91
    SciPy, 71–72, *71*, *72*
Cubic interpolation, 128–131, *129*

D

Data cleaning, 64–66, *64*, *65*, *66*
Data visualization, *See also* Matplotlib
    histograms, 78, *78*

line plots, *72*, 73–76, *73*, *74*, *75*, *76*
scatter plots, 77, *77*
DataFrame object (Pandas)
 adding columns, 61, *62*
 changing column names, 61, *62*
 Column Functions, 58–59, *59*
 DataFrame information, 59, *60*
 indexing and access, 55–58, *56*,
  57, *58*
 removing rows and columns, 60, *61*
 as a tabular structure, 55, **55**, *55*
Debian (operating system), 14, *See also*
  Raspbian (operating system)
Decision trees *See* Random forest model
Dictionaries (Python), 34–35, 54, *54*
Dilation and erosion of images,
  144–146, *145*

E

Edge detection of images, 146–148, *147*
Else in combination with while and for
  loop, 30–31, *31*
Erosion and dilation of images,
  144–146, *145*
Error (confusion) matrix, 84–85,
  84, 95
Ethernet port, 12, *13*

F

Farming and IoT, 17
For loop, 28–29, *29*, *30*

G

GPIO (general purpose input-output)
  pins, 8–9, *9*

H

HDMI (high definition multimedia
  interface) port, 10, *11*
Histograms, 78, *78*

I

IF-ELSE statements, 25–26, *26*
Image processing
 applications, 125
 bitwise operations, 134–139, *137*, *138*
 blurring and sharpening, 139–141,
  140, *141*
 brightness adjustment, 131–134,
  132, *133*
 edge detection, 146–148, *147*
 erosion and dilation, 144–146, *145*
 load, display and save an image,
  126–128, *127*
 scaling, 128–131, *129*, *130*
 segmentation using contours,
  148–150, *149*
 thresholding, 142–144, *142*, *143*
Industrial IoT, 17
Internet of things (IoT), applications, 17

K

K nearest neighbors (KNN) model,
  115–116, *115*, *116*
 advantages and limitations, 116
 example, 116–118, *118*
 model building, 92
 model training, 94
K-fold cross-validation, 83
Keyboard, connecting to, 12, 14–16, *15*, *16*

L

LibreELEC (operating system), **15**
LibreOffice suite, 14
Linalg module, 69
Line plots, *72*, 73–76, *73*, *74*, *75*, *76*
Linear discriminant analysis (LDA),
  119–120
 advantages and limitations, 120
 example, 120–121, *121*, *122*
 model building, 92
 model training, 94

Linear interpolation, 128–131, *130*
Lists (Python), 33–34, *33*
Logistic regression in machine learning, 96–97
   example, 98–99, *99*, *100*
   model building, 91
   model training, 93
   sigmoid function, 97, *97*
   types, 98
LXDE (Lightweight Desktop Environment), 14

M

Machine learning
   categories, 81–82, *82*
   classification, *See* Classification in machine learning
   k nearest neighbors (KNN) model, *See* K nearest neighbors (KNN) model
   linear discriminant analysis (LDA), *See* Linear discriminant analysis (LDA)
   Naive Bayes model, *See* Naive Bayes model
   neural network, *See* Neural network MLP
   random forest model, *See* Random forest model
   regression, *See* Regression in machine learning
   Scikit-Learn, *See* Scikit-Learn
   support vector machine (SVM), *See* Support vector machine (SVM)
Matplotlib
   histograms, 78, *78*
   installation, 73, *73*
   introduction, 72–73
   line plots, *72*, 73–76, *73*, *74*, *75*, *76*
   scatter plots, 77, *77*
Matrices, *See also* Arrays
   Cholesky decomposition, 70, *71*
   confusion (error) matrix, 84–85, *84*, 95

covariance matrix, 89–90, *89*, *90*
   inverse, 69–70, *70*
   sparsity and density, 67–68, *68*, *69*
Micro USB slot, 10, *10*
Micro-SD card slot, 12, *13*
MLP (multi-layer perceptron) *See* Neural network MLP
Monitor, connecting to, 10, 14–16, *15*, *16*
Mouse, connecting to, 12, 14–16, *15*, *16*

N

Naive Bayes model, 100–101
   advantages and applications, 101
   example, 101–102, *103*
   model building, 91
   model training, 93
Neural network MLP, 103–105, *104*
   applications, 105
   example, 105–106, *107*
   model building, 92
   model training, 93
NOOBS (new out-of-box software), 14
NumPy (numerical python)
   arrays, *See* Arrays
   data types, **38**
   overview and usage, 36, *36*

O

Operating system
   installation, 14
   LibreELEC, **15**
   Raspbian, 3, 14, **15**
   RISC OS, **15**
   Windows 10 IoT core, **15**

P

Pandas
   data cleaning, 64–66, *64*, *65*, *66*
   DataFrame object, *See* DataFrame object (Pandas)
   installation, *51*

reading CSV files, 63, *63*
Series object, *See* Series object (Pandas)
Pearson correlation, 89
Peripherals, connecting to, 10, 12, 14–16, *15, 16*
Power supply, 10
Processor, 9–10
Python, *See also* Image processing: Machine learning
  comments, 22, *22*
  conditional constructs, 25–26, *26*
  data types, 22–23, **23**, *23, 24*
  dictionaries, 34–35, 54, *54*
  keywords, 21, *21*
  libraries, **19**
    Matplotlib, *See* Matplotlib
    NumPy, *See* NumPy (numerical python)
    Pandas, *See* Pandas
    Scikit-Learn, *See* Scikit-Learn
    SciPy, *See* SciPy
  lists, 33–34, *33*
  looping constructs,
    else in combination with while and for loop, 30–31, *31*
    for loop, 28–29, *29, 30*
    while loop, 27–28, *28*
  operator precedence and associativity, 24–25, **24**
  overview, 19
  reading CSV files, *See* CSV (comma separated value) files, reading
  strings, 32–33
  ternary operator, 27, *27*
  tuples, 34
  typical program, *20*, 21
  user-defined functions, 35, *35*
  variables, 21

R

RAM, 8, 9
Random forest model, 111, **111**, *112*
  advantages and limitations, 111–112
example, 112–113, *114*
model building, 92
model training, 94
Raspberry Pi
  alternatives/competitors, **3**
  components,
    audio jack, 10, *11*
    Ethernet port, 12, *13*
    GPIO (general purpose input-output) pins, 8–9, *9*
    HDMI (high definition multimedia interface) port, 10, *11*
    Micro USB slot, 10, *10*
    micro-SD card slot, 12, *13*
    processor, 9–10
    RAM, 8, 9
    USB (universal serial bus) ports, 12, *12*
  GUI, 14
  Model, 3, 7, 8, *9*
  models (timeline), 7–8
  operating system, *See* Operating system
  philosophy, 2
  power supply, 10
Raspbian (operating system), 3, 14, **15**
Regression in machine learning, 85, *See also* Logistic regression in machine learning
Reinforcement learning, 82, *82*
Resizing images *See* Scaling images
RISC (Reduced Instruction Set Computers) architecture, 7
RISC OS, **15**
ROC (Receiver Operating Characteristic) curve, 96
  k nearest neighbors (KNN) model, *118*
  linear discrminant analysis (LDA), *122*
  logistic regression, *100*
  Naive Bayes model, *103*
  neural network MLP, *107*
  random forest model, *114*
  support vector machine (SVM), *110*
Router, connecting to, 12

S

Scaling images, 128–131, *129*, *130*
Scatter plots *See* Matplotlib: scatter plots
Scikit-Learn
    confusion (error) matrix
        implementation, 95
    example dataset, 85, **86**
    example dataset analysis, 87–88, *87*
        attributes, **86**, 88–89, *88*
        correlation, 89
        covariance matrix, 89–90,
            89, *90*
        k nearest neighbors (KNN) model,
            116–118, *118*
        linear discriminant analysis (LDA),
            120–121, *121*, *122*
        logistic regression, 98–99, *99*, *100*
        Naive Bayes model, 101–102, *103*
        neural network MLP, 105–106, *107*
        Pearson correlation, 89
        random forest model, 112–113,
            114
        support vector machine (SVM),
            109–110, *110*
    installation, 90–91, *90*
    k-fold classification accuracy, 95
    KNN model, *See* K nearest neighbors
        (KNN) model
    LDA, *See* Linear discriminant analysis
        (LDA)
    learning model building, 91
    learning model training, 92–95
    logistic regression, *See* Logistic
        regression in machine
        learning
    Naive Bayes model, *See* Naive Bayes
        model
    neural network, *See* Neural network
        MLP
    random forest model, *See* Random
        forest model
    reading CSV files, 85, *87*, 91

ROC curve, *See* ROC (Receiver
    Operating Characteristic) curve
splitting data into training and testing
    subsets, 91
SVM, *See* Support vector machine
    (SVM)
SciPy
    installation, 67
    linalg module, 69
    matrices, *See* Matrices
    reading CSV files, 71–72, *71*, *72*
Scratch, 14
Segmentation of images using contours,
    148–150, *149*
Series object (Pandas), *51*
    data cleaning, 64–66, *64*, *65*, *66*
    indexing and access, 53–54, *54*
    as Python dictionary, 54, *54*
    subarrays, 53, *53*
    for upcast, 52, *52*
Sharpening and blurring images, 139–141,
    140, *141*
Smart homes, 17
Strings (Python), 32–33
Supervised learning, 81, *82*, *See also*
    Machine learning
Support vector machine (SVM), 107–108
    applications, 108
    example, 109–110, *110*
    model building, 92
    model training, 93

T

Thresholding images, 142–144, *142*, *143*
Transformative transdisciplinary
    perspective, 2
Tuples (Python), 34

U

Unsupervised learning, 81–82, *82*
USB ports, 12, *12*

USB slot, 10, *10*
User-defined functions (Python), 35, *35*

Wi-Fi, 12
Windows 10 IoT core (operating
    system), **15**

W

Wearable devices, 17
While loop, 27–28, *28*

Printed in the United States
by Baker & Taylor Publisher Services